WORLD CHRISTIANITY

south central africa

A factual portrait of the Christian Church

MARJORIE FROISE, Editor

LCWE

MARC
A division of WORLD VISION INTERNATIONAL
919 W. Huntington Drive, Monrovia, CA 91016
Tel. (818) 303-8811

WORLD CHRISTIANITY: SOUTH CENTRAL AFRICA

Published 1991 by MARC, a division of World Vision International, 919 West Huntington Drive, Monrovia, California, 91016, U.S.A.

ISBN: 0-912552-76-X

Table of Contents

Unreached Peoples
National Churches
Foreign Missionaries
Christian Activities

Historical Background
Socioeconomic Conditions
The People
Religions
National Churches
Foreign Missionaries
Christian Activities
Rodrigues
Needs in Mauritius

Historical Background
The People
Socioeconomic Conditions
Unreached Peoples
Status of Christianity
National Churches
Foreign Missionaries
Christian Activities
Needs in Mozambique

Historical Background
The People
Socioeconomic Conditions
Status of Christianity
National Churches
Foreign Missionaries
Unreached Peoples
Christian Activities
Needs in Réunion

Historical Background

Socioeconomic Conditions
The People
Status of Christianity
National Churches
Unreached Peoples
Foreign Missionaries
Christian Activities
Needs in Seychelles

Historical Background
Socioeconomic Conditions
National Churches
Ascension
Tristan da Cunha
Status of Christianity
Needs for the Islands

Historical Background
The People
Socioeconomic Conditions
Status of Christianity
Unreached Peoples
National Churches
Foreign Missionaries
Christian Activities
Special Needs in Zambia

Historical Background
Socioeconomic Conditions
Status of Christianity
Unreached Peoples
National Churches
Foreign Missionaries
Christian Activities
Special Needs in Zimbabwe

INTRODUCTION

I was flipping through the pages of Zambia's Mindolo Ecumenical Foundation newsletter. One of the contributors ended his article with the sentence, "for those who don't know the telephone number of God and would like to contact him please ring Jeremiah 33:3." Beguiled by the dry sense of humor, I pulled out my Bible. "Call to me," I read, "and I will answer you and tell you great and unsearchable things you do not know." I was very aware before I began this research that there were many 'great and unsearchable' things I had yet to learn. At the end of the period of study I found I had only begun to scratch the surface of what I needed to know.

Possibly many of the answers are unsearchable at this time. Poor communications and road systems; the colonial legacy of comity agreements affecting networking and relationship building; the need to do thorough research of each of the countries to determine the unfinished task; all of these have a role in regulating the effectiveness and growth of the church. But there are also exciting indications that God is doing a new thing, particularly among the young people and students of Africa. This is resulting in church growth and a growing search for a deeper knowledge of God.

But there are other challenges facing the church in Africa at this time. Africa is a country of great need and the call is sounding out for Christians to be relevant in the society in which they live. Economically, food crops are declining while the population figures are rising. The challenge of food shortages, drought, warfare, displaced people and unemployment make it imperative for the church to reach out and touch hurting people and make a difference in their lives. The challenge of AIDS, spreading like a dark cloud across the sub-continent, is leaving death and orphaned children in its wake; this is the place for the church to demonstrate God's love to the world around it.

Then there is the militant Islamic push to gain control of the countries across Africa. Will Christians be onlookers in this takeover bid or will they put on the armor of God and withstand the wiles of the rulers of darkness?

Research for this book began in libraries in South Africa and I am particularly indebted to the Strange Africana library for historical information and to Africa Institute for socioeconomic data.

Libraries and archives within the countries researched added valuable insights that could not have been gained outside the country.

But it is people who have made the production of this book live. People who have given of their time to talk of their ministries, their visions and their difficulties. Sometimes it has been formal interviews, while at other times informal conversations have provided valuable observations, and little by little, a picture has emerged. Without these folk the book would never have happened.

Then there have been those closer to home who have made valuable contributions. World Vision has granted me the time to take trips away from the library to do the necessary research. My indispensable assistant, Margaret van der Merwe, has typed and retyped the pages and I thank God for her. Thank you Harald, for being so supportive, for your willingness to allow me to wander this sub-continent. Thanks also to my family who have been willing to share me with a book in the making.

But ultimately it is God who must take the glory. He has done the empowering. He has given the strength for the daily task. It is God's work out there, and I pray that this book will provide the resources that will result in church growth that many more may come to know Christ personally.

Marjorie Froise
30th May 1991

PEOPLE'S REPUBLIC OF ANGOLA

Profile

Natural features: 1,246,700 km² of land (481,354 square miles), including the enclave of Cabinda. A coastal and subplateau rising to an inland plateau with altitudes of 1,000-1,350 meters (3,280 - 4,429 feet). Jungle-covered mountains lie to the northwest.

Climate: Tropical, tempered by altitude. Coastal area arid to semi-arid. Temperatures on the inland plateau average 18°C (62°F). Rainy season from October to March. Rainfall varies from an annual average of 51 mm (2 inches) at Mocamedes on the coast to 1,780 mm (70 inches) on the northern plateau.

Population: 9.7 million (1989 est). Density: 7 people per km² (20 per square mile) (1986 est). Growth rate: 2.5%. Life expectancy: 43 years.

Ethnic groups: Three large ethnic groups, the Bakongo, Mbundu, and Ovimbundu, and about 100 tribal subgroups. 1% mestizos (mixed race), 0.3% whites. 50,000 Cubans are being repatriated.

Languages and literacy: Portuguese is the official language and also the *lingua franca*. Other languages include Umbundu (38% of population), Kimbundu (23%), Chokwe (8%), Kikonga (13.5%). Literacy rate: 30%.

Urbanization: 25% (1986 estimate). Capital city: Luanda (1.3 million in 1985). Other cities: Huambo (500,000), Lobito, Benguela.

Government: Marxist people's republic, one party state ruled by the Popular Movement for the Liberation of Angola (MPLA). Executive powers vested in President (José Eduardo dos Santos). Administrative subdivisions: Eighteen provinces.

Economy: 100 Lwei = 1 Kwanza (Kz); 60 Kz = $1 US (October 1990). GDP (1987): Kz 221.9 billion. GDP per capita (1987): US$762 Growth rate: 1973-81, negative; 1989 1-3%. Imports (1988): US $1,273m. Exports (1989): US $3,013m. Oil accounted for 89% of exports in 1986. Agriculture as a percentage of GDP: 7.8%. Agriculture employs 70-75% of economically active. Oil as a percentage of GDP: 57% (1989). Agriculture as % of GDP: 11%. Defense spending (1986): 40-50% of annual budget.

Religion: Roman Catholic 60%; Protestant 20%; Traditionalist 17%; Indigenous churches 1.5%; Atheist 1.5%.

HISTORICAL BACKGROUND

The first inhabitants of the region now called Angola were the Khoi or Bushmen, who were hunter-gatherers. Ancestors of the present population began migrating into the area from the north and east as early as 500 A.D., and settlement continued into the seventeenth century. Unlike the Khoi nomadic lifestyle, they developed subsistence settlements.

The Kongo kingdom, straddling northern Angola and Zaire, was the earliest unified empire, though it was not the biggest tribe numerically. It exerted an influence and, in some cases, control over neighboring tribes and played a major role in the slave trade. Six major ethnic groups and up to a hundred sub-groups and smaller tribes lived in the region before it became Angola, and their relationships were marked by conflict over the Kongo kingdom's designs to control and their subsequent involvement in the slave trade.

The Portuguese colonist Diogo Cão arrived in 1483. The Portugese made contact with the Kongo monarch who controlled the area at that time, and they began trading. The Portuguese rapidly gained control of the coast. A slave-trading port was established, and Portugal became a leader in the world slave trade. Permanent Portuguese settlement began in 1575, when a governor was sent to establish a garrison at Luanda.

The peoples of Angola suffered terrible oppression during the five hundred years of Portuguese rule. Between 1580 and 1913, over seven million Angolans were forced to leave their land. Only three million survived the voyage to the Americas.

The Portuguese abolished slavery in 1858, but replaced it with a system of forced labor that continued to subjugate the Angolan people well into the twentieth century. Masses of contract laborers were sent from one part of the country to another to build cities and harbors and to work on plantations. Tribes and families were separated.

At the end of the nineteenth century, the current boundaries of Angola were demarcated, dividing several of the larger ethnic groups. This resulted in problems, particularly in Northern Angola.

Since Portugal had never intended to grant its African colonies independence, it had never prepared them for self-rule. The road to independence was stormy. Three rival nationalist movements operated in different parts of the country, each drawing support from different ethnic groups.

The MPLA (*Movimento Popular de Libertacao de Angola*) originated among the Mbundu people, and soon gained support from other educated Africans and Mestizos. Its leader, Dr. Agostinho Neto, was imprisoned a number of times for political activity. In 1960, the MPLA manifesto declared its socialist aims, and over the next decade, the MPLA's Marxist ideology became evident. The movement received aid from the USSR. In 1975, when the MPLA took control of the country, Dr. Neto became Angola's first President.

The FNLA (*Frente Nacional de Libertacao de Angola*), a Kinshasa-based movement led by Holden Roberto, was supported by the Bakongo.

UNITA (National Union for Total Independence of Angola), a breakaway from FNLA, is headed by Jonas Savimbi. Originally, it represented the Ovimbundu people, but today, its sphere of influence extends beyond the Ovimbundu people. UNITA appears to hold most of Moxico, Bié, Huambo and Benguela provinces — about one-third of the country. UNITA is seeking a multi-party democracy in Angola. Its political stance is pro-Western. Although UNITA administers the area it controls, it has not established a separate government structure.

Portugal formally withdrew from Angola in August 1975, handing power to a transitional government with the understanding that a general election would take place. All three parties signed an agreement that stipulated multi-party elections. Before these elections could take place, however, the MPLA, with its strong support in Luanda, seized power.

Angola became the People's Republic of Angola in November 1975. It is a one-party state with an 11-member Political Bureau and a 65-member Central Committee.

Recent developments

Since 1976, Angola has been a politically unstable nation. The MPLA formally decided to accept Marxist-Leninist ideology one year after Portuguese withdrawal. Civil war with UNITA continued unabated for a decade, with UNITA exercising influence over large sections of the rural areas. Civil war has displaced more than one and a half million people. President dos Santos estimates that the civil war has caused $14 billion worth of damage.

A massive influx of Cubans supported the MPLA, while UNITA received support from South Africa and the United States during the years of fighting. UNITA's strategy has been to attack villages and to sabotage the economy through attacks on the infrastructure.

Although the strife in Angola started as a civil war, the presence of Cuban troops and the aggression of the South African Defence Force resulted in an escalation of the war to the extent that it became a regional conflict which could not be resolved between the combatants in Angola alone.

A crucial turning point came in July 1988, when Angolan, Cuban, and South African delegations agreed on a comprehensive settlement that recognized the importance of the Namibian issue. Namibian independence in 1990, the return of an estimated 50,000 Cubans, and the withdrawal of the SADF paved the way for talks to end the fifteen year war. In June 1989, the Angolan government and UNITA agreed to a ceasefire.

At a congress in April 1991, the MPLA put aside Marxist-Leninism in favor of a social democracy. A peace accord will be signed by both factions, and multi-party elections will be held in 1992.

SOCIOECONOMIC CONDITIONS

Angola is potentially one of the richest countries in Africa. Large deposits of oil and gas are the mainstay of the economy, representing more than 90 percent of its foreign trade revenue. Diamonds are mined, and their potential is relatively untapped.

Despite these resources, Angola is struggling economically. The exodus of 90 percent of Portuguese settlers at independence created a crisis in skilled labor, and economic activity is slower than it was in the early seventies. This loss of skill has been exacerbated by the drain of potential workers into the defense force. President dos Santos has announced plans to decentralize economic planning and encourage private enterprise, but many Angolans feel that political stability is an indispensable condition for economic recovery.

Health

Cuban and Russian medical teams provide up to a third of healthcare services, but some 70 percent of Angolans have no access to health services, and the number is increasing. About 40-45 percent of children suffer from moderate malnutrition. An estimated 1.9 million people are affected by famine in the south of central Angola. Angola's infant mortality rate is one of the highest in the world. About 20,000 people have lost limbs, mainly through detonating anti-personnel mines. Five overseas trained doctors and 3,500 trained nurses staff a 200-bed hospital in Jamba.

Agriculture

Angola has vast agricultural potential. Arable land comprises 24 percent of land area, but only 2-3 percent is currently used. Because of widespread insecurity, an increasing number of farmers have left their villages to migrate to safer urban areas. Food production has been cut in half since independence, and more than 80 percent of food consumed is imported, mainly in the form of aid from Western countries. About 1.4 million people are severely affected by food shortages. The people buy food in government stores using ration cards. An encouraging harvest of maize in the 1986-87 season, however, met 68 percent of local needs.

Education

In UNITA-controlled areas, education is offered up to Standard 9 (Grade 11) in Portuguese. About 500 students study abroad.

Table 1: SOCIAL INDICATORS IN BRIEF

Primary school age children in school	66%
Secondary school age children in school	2%
Pupil teacher ratio	58:1
Adult literacy rate	30%
Population per doctor	13,723
Population per hospital bed	322
Infant mortality rate	200 per 1,000
Life expectancy	43 years

THE PEOPLE

In 1970, 5.62 million people lived in Angola. The current estimate (1988) is 9.4 million. The 1970 census, which is the last one taken, did not provide ethnic breakdowns. The most recent data on ethnicity comes from the 1960 census, which indicated that 75 percent of the population are in four large ethnolinguistic groups, each with a number of subgroups.

The largest group is the Ovimbundu (language Umbundu) which accounts for 38 percent of the population. Most Ovimbundu live in the central southern provinces of Kwanza Sul, Benguela, Huambo, Bié and Huila.

The Mbundu group (language Kimbundu) accounts for 23 percent of the population. They live in the central provinces of Luanda, Bengo, Kwanza Norte and Kwanza Sul.

The Bakongo (language Kikongo) live in the northern provinces of Cabinda, Uige and Mbanza Kongo and constitute 13.5 percent of the population.

Other groups include Lunda-Chokwe in the eastern provinces (8%), the Ovambo people in the south (2.5%), the Nhaneca-Humbe (5%) in the south, and the Nganguela (7%), made up of twenty subgroups in the southeast.

An estimated 7,000 San people (Bushmen) belong to three tribes. The San were the original inhabitants of the area but have been pushed into the Namibe Desert.

Altogether, about a hundred tribes live in Angola, with languages different enough to allow each to be classified as a separate people. A number of ethnic groups live in areas that span borders with neighboring countries.

At independence, about 500,000 Europeans (mostly Portuguese) lived in Angola, but today that number has shrunk to 40,000. There are 150,000 Angolans of mixed descent. Fifty thousand Cubans who were in Angola because of the war are being repatriated.

Angola currently has a displaced population of 1,533,000 and hosts a number of refugees from countries in Southern Africa.

Portuguese is the official language of Angola. None of the African languages extend beyond their ethnic area, and Portuguese is the only language that can be used countrywide.

STATUS OF CHRISTIANITY

Early church history

To the early Portuguese navigators who arrived in 1483, the introduction of Catholicism was an integral part of colonial policy. In 1491, the Portuguese established the first Catholic mission to Angola in the north. Jesuits, Capuchins, and Carmelites were the first to evangelize the area.

The king of the ruling Kongo kingdom accepted Christianity. His son became the first African bishop, and the church grew rapidly. This early growth was not sustained for two main reasons. First, malaria and dysentery killed many priests. By the middle of the nineteenth century, only five priests remained in Angola. Second, when the slave trade was flourishing, bishops and priests baptized groups of slaves before the slaves were shipped to foreign lands. This involvement in the slave trade caused the people to become disillusioned with the church. It was not until the late nineteenth century that the church began to establish itself, beginning to work in the interior of Angola.

The first Protestants in Angola were British Baptists, who arrived in 1878 to work among the Bakongo people in the north. Shortly after their arrival, the American Board Mission sent a party to work among the Ovimbundu. In 1884, the Brethren Mission began its work, pioneered by Frederick Arnot. Other early entrants were William Taylor and his party from America, who founded the United Methodist Church, Rev. Stober, who founded the Evangelical Mission of Angola, and Heli Chatelain of the Swiss Mission, who founded the Philafricaine Mission in 1897.

These missionaries faced many discouragements. The death toll from malaria was high. Numerous tombstones at mission stations bear witness to the dedication of these early workers.

As churches and missions were organized, they established denominational patterns in the villages. A village would be composed of groups of people, each with their own identities, either Catholic, Protestant, or traditional. Conversions to different sects of Christianity created new systems of local authority. Comity agreements between Protestant denominations resulted in denominational differences between tribes.

Under Portuguese rule

Under Portuguese rule, Angola was a Catholic country. Although the constitution allowed for freedom of worship, the Catholic church enjoyed a privileged status, and Protestant churches found it difficult to gain official recognition. Discrimination against the Protestant church was evident.

In 1961, the struggle for independence compounded difficulties between the two denominations since the leaders of all three nationalist movements were sons of Protestant church leaders. Many Protestant churches were closed and missionaries expelled, particularly Baptists and Methodists working in the north. Several pastors were killed or imprisoned, and church work was gravely hindered.

Christianity today

The last official record of religious affiliation was the 1950 census, which recorded that 36 percent of the population was Catholic and 13 percent was Protestant. The takeover by the Marxist government in 1974 brought many changes to the country and to the church.

Article 7 of the Constitution states that the People's Republic of Angola is a secular state with complete separation between state and religious institutions. All religions are to be respected and the State will give its protection to churches and places of worship, provided they conform to the laws of the State. The law furthermore guarantees equality of all faiths. Because of the civil war, Marxist philosophy has never been systematically applied, and government attitudes towards the church have depended largely on the governor of a particular area.

Tribalism is discouraged by the MPLA government. Since UNITA also discourages tribalism and supports Protestant Christianity, traditional religion is being squeezed out in all areas of the country.

Despite some difficulties, the post-colonial church has grown and is now far stronger than when the country was under Portuguese rule. Although many people initially turned away from Christianity at independence, most of those who defected have returned to their churches. Protestant churches have seen a dramatic period of consolidation and rapid growth. Since 1982, Christians have become more aggressive in their outreach.

In January 1987, the Ministry of Justice passed an executive decree recognizing major denominations. Twelve churches were listed, and since then, another has been added. Recognized denominations include:

- Assemblies of God
- Baptist Convention
- Congregational Church of Angola
- Evangelical Baptist Church
- Evangelical Church of Angola
- Evangelical Church of South West Angola
- Evangelical Reformed Church in Angola
- Kimbanguist Church in Angola
- Roman Catholic Church
- Seventh Day Adventist church
- Simao Toko
- Union of Evangelical Churches
- United Methodist Church

Although not specifically mentioned in the 1987 decree, parachurch organizations like the Bible Society also came under its jurisdiction since they exist to serve the churches. Many churches, however, were not included in the decree, a number of which had sprung up since independence. Twenty churches were officially banned and closed. Small or newly established groups are encouraged to join recognized churches. Others have received some hope of recognition from the government.

The 1960 census showed that Angola is 51 percent Catholic, 17 percent Protestant and 32 percent "nonreligious" (a term that included traditional religions). Current religious statistics are very difficult to obtain because of the breakdown in communications. Figures given, therefore, are broad estimates.

Table 2: Religious Affiliation in Angola [1]

Roman Catholic	60.0%

Protestant	20.0%
Traditional	17.0%
Atheists	1.5%
Indigenous churches	1.5%

[1] United Bible Society estimate

NATIONAL CHURCHES

Cooperation between Protestant missions in Angola resulted in the formation of the Evangelical Alliance in 1928. Despite a number of requests to the Portuguese government, the association failed to gain official recognition.

Today, two coordinating bodies draw churches together. The Angolan Council of Evangelical Churches (CAIE) was founded in 1977. The Council seeks to promote unity among churches and represents them at national and international levels. It provides relief, trains leaders, and encourages the production of Christian literature. Affiliated members in 1985 were:

- African Apostolic Church
  (Igreja Apostolica Africana)
- Church Full of the Word of God
  (Igreja Cheia da Palavra de Deus)
- Evangelical Baptist Church
  (Igreja Evangelica Baptista)
- Evangelical Church of Angola
  (Igreja Evangelica de Angola)
- Evangelical Church of the
  Apostles of Jerusalem
  (Igreja Evangelica dos Apostolos de Jerusalem)
- Evangelical Congregational Church
  (Igreja Evangelica Congregacional)
- Evangelical Pentecostal Mission in Angola
  (Missao Evangelica Pentecostal em Angola)
- Evangelical Reformed Church of Angola
  (Igreja Evangelica Reformada de Angola)
- Kimbanguist Church in Angola
  (Igreja Kimbanguista em Angola)
- United Evangelical Church in Angola
  (Igreja Evangelica Unida em Angola)
- United Methodist Church
  (Igreja Metodista Unida)

The Association of Evangelicals (AEA), founded in 1974, represented about 60 percent of Protestants at the time of independence. About 18 percent of the total population were Protestants.

The AEA maintains that at independence, more than half the Protestants in the country were evangelical in belief and alignment. Of the churches in the AEA, four have received official recognition, and six are waiting for registration.

Members of the AEA are:

- Igreja Evangelica do Sudoeste de Angola
- Igreja Evangelica Luterana do Sul de Angola
- Igreja Crista Evangelica
- Igreja Evangelica dos Irmaos em Angola
- Igreja Evangelica Pentecostal em Angola
- Convencao Baptista de Angola
- Uniao de Igregas Evanglicas de Angola
- Igreja de Cristo em Angola
- Igreja Presbiteriana em Angola

Table 3: ESTABLISHED CHURCHES IN ANGOLA
WITH AVAILABLE MEMBERSHIP STATISTICS

Roman Catholics (1983) [1]	3,307,200
United Methodist Church of Angola	120,000
Evangelical Church of the Brethren in Angola	100,000
Evangelical Congregational Church in Angola	100,000
Seventh Day Adventists	85,000
Council of Evangelical Churches of Central Africa	80,000
Assemblies of God Pentecostals of Angola	60,000
Evangelical Baptist Church in Angola (1987) [2]	47,000
Evangelical Church of South West Angola	40,000
Union of Evangelical Churches in Angola	30,000
Evangelical Church of Angola (1987) [2]	25,000
Baptist Convention of Angola (1985)	20,400
Church of God — Cleveland (1984)	20,000
Evangelical Pentecostal Church of Angola	19,000
United Evangelical Church of Angola	11,000
Evangelical Lutheran Church	6,000
Christian Evangelical Church	5,000
Church of Christ in Angola	5,000
Presbyterian Church of Angola	2,500
Church in the Bush of Angola	
Evangelical Reformed Church of Angola	
Kimbanguist Church in Angola	
Philafricaine Church	
Salvation Army	

[1] *Baptized members but not necessarily practicing members.*
[2] *Includes adherents and children.*

Roman Catholic Church

The Roman Catholic Church in Angola was closely associated with the colonial powers before independence. Staff of the Catholic teachers' training colleges were expected to be Portuguese since Portuguese was the language of instruction in mission schools. Portuguese bishops believed that "the role of the church was to safeguard the very soul of this civilization and to transmit its basic values."[1]

The close relationship between the church and the Portuguese regime made it difficult for the church to establish a positive relationship with the new government. After an initial period of hardship, the church is again beginning to re-establish itself. The Catholic population is strongest among the Ovimbundu of Central Angola. In 1970, the concentration of Roman Catholics in Benguela was about 80 percent, while in the Luso area, the figure was as low as 15 percent.

In 1966, the Roman Catholic Church in Angola was divided into six diocese. In 1967, there were 839 Catholic primary schools, 24 secondary schools, 11 hospitals, 108 dispensaries and clinics, and 20 maternity centers in the country. By 1973, the church supported 1,641 primary schools (176,000 pupils) and 47 secondary schools (6,399 pupils). Education was taken over by the government at independence.

More recently, the church has grown rapidly. By 1983, about 50 percent of the population had become Catholic. Of Angola's eleven bishops, ten are Angolan and one Portuguese. Of 312 priests, 38 percent are Angolan, and 34 percent of nuns are Angolan. The number of students in major seminaries increased from 123 to 135 and novice sisters from 52 to 81. In UNITA-held territories, however, the number of Roman Catholics is shrinking.

Protestant churches

EVANGELICAL CONGREGATIONAL CHURCH IN ANGOLA
(IGREJA EVANGELICA CONGREGACIONAL EM ANGOLA)

This church was established by the American Board Mission, whose missionaries landed in Benguela in 1880, and the United Church of Canada, who began a ministry in 1886. Due to comity agreements between different Protestant denominations, it has a

---

1   Pro Mundi Vita centrum information, *Government policies and the church in the Portuguese territories of Africa.*

strong following in the central and southern parts of the country. Before independence, the church was African-controlled, and supported 70 pastors who were assisted by 56 expatriate workers.

Since independence, the church has been torn by the civil war. Some members seek ties with the government and the rest support UNITA. Most members are Ovimbundu, the largest ethnolinguistic group in Uganda.

This denomination is deeply involved in social activity. At independence, the church operated seven hospitals and an extensive rural health service. Its renowned training center at Dondi for both theological and technical training was destroyed during the civil war. Pastors are now trained in an interdenominational (CAIE) seminary in Huambo.

EVANGELICAL BAPTIST CHURCH IN ANGOLA
(IGREJA EVANGELICA BAPTISTA EM ANGOLA)

The Evangelical Baptist Church in Angola was formed in 1961 and drew together the work of British, Canadian and Independent Baptists.

George Grenfell and Thomas Comber, British Baptist missionaries, were the first Protestant missionaries to establish a work in Angola. They arrived in 1878 in the northern region, and planted churches that spread from Sao Salvador throughout the Bakongo region. The missionaries avoided Westernized forms of worship, but encouraged newly-formed churches to develop their own forms of worship, using the Bible as their rule and guide. The 1950 census indicated that 35 percent of the population of Uige and the neighboring Zaire district was Protestant.

Mathew Stober of the Angolan Evangelical Mission started the work of the Canadian Baptists in 1897. Portuguese Baptists, who arrived in 1929, have planted eight small churches.

According to the 1960 census, the Bakongo ethno-linguistic people, who live in the area where most Baptists work, were thoroughly saturated by the gospel. Some 46 percent claimed to be Catholic, 32 percent Protestant, and only 12 percent non-Christian.

In 1961, when the Bakongo region in the north was declared a military zone, ten Baptist missions were in the area. Because of military operations, most of the stations were closed or carried on minimally. Many Christians fled into neighboring Zaire. When they returned to northern Angola at independence, only two of their 240 churches were still standing.

After independence, churches grew rapidly. By 1982, more than 20,000 communicants and a further 27,000 children and affiliates attended. Scattered church fellowships came together to form the Evangelical Baptist Church in Angola (IEBA). Some 155 pastors and evangelists, both clergy and laity, care for the people.

The Baptist Convention of Angola, with 60 churches and a membership of 20,420, is strongest in the North (Uige), and in Central Angola (Huambo).

UNITED METHODIST CHURCH
(IGREJA METODISTA UNIDA)

In 1855, William Taylor of the Methodist Episcopal Church in America arrived in Luanda with 30 missionaries in his pioneering band. They penetrated 350 miles to Malanje, where they established five mission stations.

Early days were difficult. By the turn of the century, of the 86 missionaries who had been sent, 11 were dead and 55 had returned home discouraged. The work gradually grew more stable as Malanje and Luanda became the two principal areas of missionary activity.

The Methodist church encouraged the development of independent churches. Churches flourished in the city of Luanda and in its outskirts, and by 1961 there were 22 churches in the area. In the same year, Methodists cared for more than 5,000 children in 99 schools. By 1967, 41 Methodist circuits operated in five districts. At independence, church members numbered 42,000. Since then, the denomination has grown rapidly and includes about 120,000 members. The church is led by an Angolan bishop.

EVANGELICAL CHURCH OF THE BRETHREN IN ANGOLA
(CHRISTIAN MISSIONS IN MANY LANDS)

Frederick Arnot arrived in 1884 to pioneer the work among the Chokwe-Lunda people. The Chokwe were unresponsive at first, but Arnot and his team persevered. By 1958, the gospel was being preached in 150 villages with more than 6,000 believers in fellowship. Adherents were estimated to number a further 10,000.

The Brethren Assemblies also established churches among the Ovimbundu people. By 1958, 7,500 believers formed 50 assemblies in the Bié district. In the district of Luanda, lay leaders established about a hundred assemblies.

At independence, Brethren Assemblies administered six primary schools, two hospitals and two leprosaria. By 1981, only eight expatriate missionaries remained in the country, down from 58 in earlier days. Total membership today is about 100,000.

UNION OF EVANGELICAL CHURCHES
(UNIAO DE IGREJAS EVANGELICAS DE ANGOLA)

South African General Mission, which is now the Africa Evangelical Fellowship, entered Angola in 1914. William Bailey was the team leader and began work among the Ganguela people (Luimbe, Luena, Bundu, Lutchazi). One of their main stations was

Catota, where they established a hospital and Bible school. This mission station was eventually destroyed during the civil war.

This church has been hit hard by the fighting. Churches in the southeast are cut off from churches in the southwest. Many Christians have fled into northern Namibia or Zambia.

In 1983, there were 4,500 members and a further 20,000 adherents. The church community is cared for by 14 full-time pastors and 35 part-time workers. The current estimate of church membership is 30,000.

Leadership training, which these churches see as a pressing need, takes place in Portuguese at the Theological Seminary at Lubango. A Bible School at Menongue trains pastors in vernacular languages.

EVANGELICAL CHURCH OF SOUTHWEST ANGOLA
(IGREJA EVANGELICA DO SUDOESTE DE ANGOLA)

In 1897, Heli Chatelain founded the Evangelical Church of Southwest Angola (IESA) at Caluquembe. In 1908 it was taken over by the Swiss Reformed Church and became known as Mission Philafricaine. In 1967, Mission Philafricaine was officially renamed Alliance Missionnaire Evangelique (AME). It operates in the Benguela, Huila and Namibe provinces.

This denomination, with a communicant membership of 40,000, is deeply involved in social work. In 1974, seven mission stations were responsible for four hospitals, a nursing school, three leprosaria, 20 primary schools and two secondary schools. AME's ministry is mainly to the Ovimbundu people in three provinces.

THE EVANGELICAL CHURCH OF ANGOLA IN THE BUSH

This church developed in a UNITA-controlled area in the southeastern part of Angola. Although the majority of members originally come from Brethren and Congregational churches, it is a nondenominational body controlled by a Christian Council of Churches. The community is divided into 13 congregations, each with a number of outstations. There is a constant call for Christian literature, such as Bibles in national languages, song books for the congregations, and commentaries to train pastors.

Pentecostal churches

In 1939, Pearl and Mabel Stark of the United States arrived in Angola and established the Pentecostal Mission. After Pearl Stark's untimely death, his wife asked the Assemblies of God in Portugal for help. As a result, the Pentecostal Mission was eventually consolidated under the ministry of the Assemblies of God.

Portuguese persecution forced expatriates out of Angola during the fifties. During those 14 years of persecution, the Assemblies of God church grew. The work is now separated into three churches: Assemblies of God, the Evangelical Pentecostal Church, and the Evangelical Pentecostal Mission of Angola

African independent churches

Independent churches have never had a strong following in Angola, initially because of clampdowns by the Portuguese government.

In 1921, the Kimbanguist Church was founded by Simon Kimbangu in Zaire. Kimbangu's followers believed the Holy Spirit had descended upon him, giving him power to heal and preach. They practiced baptism and purification rites. Kimbangu was committed to life imprisonment and died in 1951 after spending many years in solitary confinement. His teachings, however, lived on and spread across Zaire and into Angola. The Kimbanguist Church is now a registered church in Angola.

Simao Toco prophesied about a new era in which Toco was the last prophet. Although he was banned by the Belgian Congo and exiled to the south by the Portuguese, his teaching continued to spread and became a movement. It was banned by the MPLA government, but its suppression has since been reversed and it is now a recognized church.

Other groups include the African Church, the Betania Church, the Church of the Apostles, and Church of Blacks.

Traditional religion

Throughout history, most Angolans have believed in an omnipotent creator who is the ultimate cause of all things. In their traditions, he is unknowable and cannot be approached directly. He is known as Suku or Nzambi, or as Kalunga in the southwest.

Traditionalists ask the spirits of their deceased ancestors for help at harvest time and when unexplained misfortunes like famines strike. Ancestors are appeased through gifts and rituals. The most important ancestors are those of the mother's kin. Diviners, medicine men, or sorcerers also are approached for help. Fetishes and charms are considered to be conductors of supernatural powers.

Some who profess Christianity blend their faith with traditional religion. For these, only a few elements of Christianity are added to tribal religion in varying degrees.

FOREIGN MISSIONARIES

Protestant missionary societies have been involved in church-planting in Angola since 1878, when British Baptist missionaries arrived in northern Angola. Other missionary societies followed, and by 1960, about 260 missionaries worked in Angola. During the civil war, Portuguese rule became oppressive and many missions withdrew. The number of missionaries dropped from 260 to below 70 in 1966, to only 36 in 1972. Today there are 50 missionaries, 30 of whom are involved in medical work.

Under MPLA rule, missionaries are permitted to enter Angola only if requested by a recognized national church. They work with the national churches in medical work, training programs, development, and aid programs. Missions currently represented in Angola include:

- African Evangelical Fellowship
- Alliance Missionaire Evangelique
- Assemblies of God
- Baptist Missionary Society (UK)
- Christian Mission in Many Lands
- ICCO (Dutch)
- Reformed Church of Scotland
- South Baptist Convention

In addition to the missionary organizations working in Angola, a number of para-church organizations are involved in ministry. These include:

- Caritas
- Gospel Recordings
- Interchurch Aid Commission
- International Fellowship of Evangelical Students (IFES)
- Project Timothy
- Scripture Union

UNREACHED PEOPLES

Many pockets of people are still unevangelized. Communication has broken down because of the war. Those who attempt road travel do so at great risk. Generally, people in the north have had more exposure to Christianity than people in the rest of the country.

The 7,000 San (Bushmen) living in remote arid areas are totally unreached.

The Nganguela people, in their many subgroups, have had little Christian witness and are predominantly traditionalists.

The Nyaneka-Humbe people in the Huila province are unreached. UIEA and the IESA churches are reaching out to them.

Va Bukusu (Mbukushu) live in the southeast. This people group extends into Botswana and Namibia, where Christians are trying new initiatives to bring the gospel to them.

Christians are also starting work with the Quipungu people in the south. Other groups in the country include the Va Gambwe, Va Kuvale, Va Ndombe, Va Cilenge Musio.

Two other groups of unreached people are the ruling party, with 33,000 members dedicated to Marxist-Leninist ideology, and the Cubans still in the country, working in the military, education, or health. Several thousand Russian and Eastern European advisors also live in the country.

Political instability in Angola over the past two decades has created a large refugee population. As a result, cities and suburbs have grown rapidly. So many new urban churches have sprung up that most church work today is in towns or cities. Urban areas like Luanda have become so diverse that it is difficult for pastors to minister to people in their own languages.

CHRISTIAN ACTIVITIES

Evangelism

Churches are growing as Angolan Christians share the good news of Jesus Christ with others. In 1983, a Brazilian evangelist conducted the first series of evangelistic crusades permitted since independence, and many came to know the Lord. International Fellowship of Evangelical Students (IFES) conducts evangelism and discipleship courses.

Radio

- The Roman Catholic Church had two radio stations at Nova Lisboa and Radio Ecclesia in Luanda which were taken over by the government in 1978. Today, Vatican Radio has a Portuguese service beamed to Angola.
- Trans World Radio currently presents programs, mainly in Portuguese and Umbundu.
- The Evangelical Church of Southwest Angola established a small studio in 1978 in Kalukembe that enables them to produce programs locally.
- The religious service of the national radio service in Namibia produces programs for refugees in northern Namibia and southern Angola.

- FEBA broadcasts programs to Mozambique and Angola. Production and response to these broadcasts is chanelled through Radio Mission and Brethren Assemblies.
- HCJB/World Radio Missionary Fellowship transmits programs in Portuguese. They report that many letters of response are received from young people in particular.

Scripture translation

Missionary societies entering Angola at the end of the last century and early this century recognized the need to put major languages in writing and translate Scriptures into these languages. A number of missionaries were involved in linguistic and translation work. Heli Chatelain, a linguist who arrived in Angola in 1885 from Switzerland, took only three years to learn Kimbundu, prepare a grammar, and produce a dictionary. William and Wesley Stover provided a vocabulary and grammar for the Umbundu people and translated the New Testament.

In 1888, the Gospel of John was translated, and in 1922 the New Testament was available. The first Scripture in Kikongo was also published in 1888, the New Testament in 1893 and the complete Bible in 1916. The first Umbundu Scripture portion was published in 1897 and the first Chokwe Scripture in 1916.

The Nkhumbi people living in the south of Angola recently received 15,000 copies of the Gospel of John, the first written work to appear in their language.

Projects to revise the Kikongo and Umbundu Scriptures have been delayed because of unrest.

The complete Bible has been translated into the following languages: Tchokwe, Herero, Kikongo, Kimbundu, Kwanyama, Umbundu, Ngangela, Lovale, Kuanyama, Nyemba, Ndonga, Luchazi and Songo. Portions of Scripture exist in Lumuila, Lunyaweka, Luhanda, Luchazi, Lunda, Luvale, Umbundu and Mbunda.

The Bible Society distributes Scriptures in Kikongo, Kimbundu, Tchokwe, Umbundu, Luvale, Portuguese, Spanish and Russian. Gospels are distributed in Songo and Nkhumbi. In 1987, 103,889 Bibles, 21,536 New Testaments and 58,258 portions were distributed. The Bible Society reports that despite communication difficulties caused by the war, Scriptures are distributed on shoulders, bicycles, trucks, and even airplanes.

The Bible Society's greatest problem is the foreign exchange regulation that prevents the export of local currency to buy more Bibles. Since Bibles cannot be imported, all Bibles coming into the country must be donated.

Christian literature

The American Board Mission established a printing press at Camundongo for the Umbundu people. Later, the mission set up another one at Donde for the Umbundu, and one at Boma for the Chokwe people.

In 1922, new regulations hampered the production and use of Christian literature. The Portuguese government decreed that all instruction in mission schools should be in Portuguese, and the "use of the native language in written form by means of pamphlets, papers or whatever kind of manuscript (was) forbidden. Books for religious teaching (were) not permitted in any language other than Portuguese."[2] They did, however, allow material to be printed in dual languages during an interim period. Bilingual publication of material added greatly to the cost but production continued.

Restrictions regarding the use of Portuguese have now been lifted. Today most of the material used in evangelism and teaching is sent in from outside the country. Agencies involved in literature work report an overwhelming need for Christian literature. Many Christians lost Bibles, hymnals and other Christian literature while fleeing the civil war.

The government's literacy campaign has produced new readers eager to find something to read. Christians have the opportunity to give these newly-literate people Scriptures and teaching material. Church leaders emphasize the need for Christian literature, and have called for agencies to assist in producing literature in local languages for Christians as well as for outreach and evangelism.

All Nations Gospel Publishers publishes Bibles, New Testaments, books and tracts in Umbundu, Chokwe, Kimbundu, Ngangela and Portuguese. Christian Missions in Many Lands (Brethren) sends Emmaus correspondence courses and other literature to isolated believers throughout Angola. IESA continues to produce Christian literature and has translated material into languages such as Nkhumbi and Quipungu in the south. Scripture Union in Angola produces notes in Portuguese, Umbundu and Kokongo, and has distributed 20,000 Scripture Union notes in Angola. Gospel Printing Mission distributes Portuguese tracts. Scripture Gift Mission portions are being distributed.

---

2   U.S. Government Printing Office, *Area Handbook for Angola 1967*.

In the southern part of Angola, a number of Christian organizations distribute Christian literature throughout Namibia, and particularly to UNITA-controlled areas.

Christian education

The need for trained leadership is great. Few people have much education and the church needs more well-trained leaders. Bible seminaries and schools currently in Angola include:

- Escola Biblica Kaluquembe
- Curro Para Formacao de Obreiros in Luanda
- Escola de Biblica de Kessua in Malange (Methodist Church of Angola)
- Instituto Biblico Baptista
- Instituto Biblico in Cabinda
- Instituto Biblico de Menongue (assisted by the Africa Evangelical Fellowship)
- Instituto Biblico de Shangalala in Xangongo
- Seminario Emanuel Unido in Huambo (serving the Congregational, Methodist and Reformed Churches)
- Seminario Sao Jose Clony in Malanje (trains Roman Catholics for priesthood)
- Seminario Theologico de Lubango (supported by the Association of Evangelicals; offers four year courses in Portuguese)
- Seminario Tedogico Baptista, in Huambo

In addition, Brethren and Evangelical churches offer correspondence courses. A number of students study in countries outside Angola, particularly Brazil.

Social work

Since the earliest years, Angola's churches have cared for their congregations by providing educational and medical facilities. Portuguese authorities required that each mission station provide schooling and medical care for the Angolan people.

The Catholic church tended to concentrate on education. By 1966, they were responsible for 1,537 primary schools and 25 high schools, amounting to 75 percent of the total number of schools in Angola. The church was also responsible for nine hospitals and 55 dispensaries.

Protestant churches administered 14 hospitals and a large number of clinics and leprosaria. Education also played a major role in the ministry before independence.

At independence, the government took over the education system. Many of the hospitals and health care centers have been closed down because of civil disruption.

A generation of Angolans has known no other life than war. Refugees and displaced persons from rural areas arrive in the cities and towns in search of security. Churches are working together among these refugees to provide vocational and skills training centers. The Angolan Council of Churches (C.A.I.E.), the Roman Catholic Church, and the Association of Evangelicals of Angola are the main channels of aid from churches and agencies overseas.

BIBLIOGRAPHY

Abshire, David M. and Samuels, M.A, *Portuguese Africa: A Handbook*, Center for Strategic Studies, Georgetown University, USA.

ACTEA, *ACTEA Directory of Theological Schools in Africa*.

Barrett, David, *World Christian Encyclopedia*, Oxford University Press.

Baron, Alan, *Crisis in Angola: Problems and Prospects*, SAF No. 2 1988.

Economist Intelligence Unit, *Angola E10 Country Report* No. 1, 1991.

Economist Intelligence Unit, *Angola Country Profile 1990/91*.

Henderson, Lawrence W., *Angola: Five Centuries of Conflict*, Cornell University, 1979.

Hodges, Tony, *Angola to the 1990's: The Potential for Recovery*, Economist Intelligence Unit.

Kane, J. Herbert, *A Global View of Christian Missions*, Baker.

Kreuth, Wildbad, *Regional Implications in Angola and Namibia*, Africa Institute Bulletin, Vol. 28, No. 10, 1988.

Okuma, Thomas, *The Social Response of Christianity in Angola*, Boston University Graduate School.

Parsons, Robert T (Editor), *Windows on Africa*, Brill Leiden, 1971.

Somerville, Keith, *Angola: Politics, Economics and Society*, Pinters Publishers, 1986.

Trans World Radio, *Country Report*.

United Bible Societies, *Angola Bulletin*, First/Second quarters, 1988.

United States of America Department of State, *Background Notes*, Angola, 3/85.

U.S. Government Printing Office, *Area Handbook for Angola*, 1979.

World Council of Churches, "Survey on Angola," *Handbook of Member Churches*, November 1986.

FEDERAL ISLAMIC REPUBLIC OF THE COMOROS

Profile

Natural Features: Comoros is a volcanic archipelago with four main islands and many smaller islands between the African coast and Madagascar. Total land area is 1,862 km² (719 sq. miles): Grande Comore (Njazidja), 1,148 km² (443 square miles) Anjouan (Nzwani), 424 km² (163 square miles); and Mohe'li (Mwali), 290 km² (112 square miles). Terrain varies from island to island. Grande Comore is marked by steep mountains, with Kartala, an active volcano, as the island's highest peak at 2,361 meters (7,750 feet).

Climate: The climate is tropical, with a hot rainy season from November to March. Climate, rainfall and vegetation differ from island to island.

Population: The 1980 census recorded a total population of 335,150: Grand Comore, 242,000; Anjouan, 146,000; Mohéli, 18,000. Population estimate for 1990 was 423,000. About 100,000 Comorians live outside of Comoros. Population density: 232 per km² (602 per square mile), but this varies from island to island. Life expectancy: 55 years. The average annual population growth rate was 3.7% between 1980 and 1985.

Languages and literacy: Comoros' official language was French until independence, when it was changed to Arabic. In reality, Arabic is seldom spoken, and French remains the language of commerce and government. The majority of the people speak Comorian, a mixture of Arabic and Swahili. There are a number of Comorian dialects. Shingazidja is spoken on Grande Comore, Shimwali on Mohéli, Shinzwani on Anjouan and Shimaore on Mayotte. Malagasy is also spoken. About 60 percent of the people are literate.

Urbanization: 12% (1980). Urbanization growth rate: 7.5% per year. Principal towns: Moroni (capital) 22,000; Mutsamudu 14,000; Fomboni 5,400 (1980 census).

Government: The islands of Grand Comore, Anjouan and Mohéli are governed by the Federal Islamic Republic of the Comoros. The island of Mayotte is under French rule.

Economy: 100 centimes = 1 Comorian franc. Exchange rate: 318 Comorian francs = US$1 (average for 1989). The Comorian franc has a fixed link to the French franc (1Ff = 50 Cf). GDP 1988: Cf 61.28 billion; GDP per capita: Cf 13.776. Imports (1989): US$ 44.3m. Exports: US$ 21.5m. Agriculture accounts for 34% of GDP (1987) and 95% of export earnings. Some 50% of the population is employed in agriculture. Growth rate averaged 2% a year between 1981 and 1985; in 1988, 0.7%.

Religion: Muslim 99%; Catholics and Protestants 1% (including expatriates).

HISTORICAL BACKGROUND

The first settlers on the islands were probably Melano-Polynesians who arrived in the sixth century. Between the 10th and 15th centuries, waves of Shirazi Muslim refugees fled the Red Sea area and settled on the islands of Comoros, establishing sultanates. Islam became a unifying force that dominated Comorian life for many centuries.

In 1841, the French landed on Mayotte. The ruling sultan agreed to cede Mayotte to the French, and the other islands gradually came under French rule. In 1912, Comoros was declared a French colony.

Between 1914 and 1946, Comoros was administered by Madagascar. France did not try to develop the islands, and Comorians continued in their traditional way of life.

In 1961, France granted the islands of Comoros a system of internal autonomy. The desire for independence grew, and the years between 1971 and 1973 were full of political turmoil. A referendum was held in December 1974, and 94 percent of Comorians voted in favor of independence. The people of Mayotte dissented, voting overwhelmingly in favor of remaining a French colony.

In 1975, Comoros declared its independence from France. Ahmed Abdallah was elected the first president. The Islamic Republic of Comoros was admitted to the United Nations, and the General Assembly confirmed the Republic's authority over the island of Mayotte.

A coup led by Ali Soilih overthrew Abdallah soon after his installation, and led to three years of uncertainty and disarray. With the help of mercenaries, Abdallah was reinstated in 1978, and his leadership was reinforced by the people through a referendum and subsequent elections. In November 1989, Abdallah was assassinated, and an interim government was installed and subsequently confirmed by ballot.

THE PEOPLE

People originating in many different countries live on the islands of Comoros. By the 16th century, people from Africa, Indonesia, Madagascar and the Middle East had joined the original Melano-Polynesian settlers. Europeans, mainly Portuguese, Dutch and French, added to the ethnic complexity.

Each island has its own traditions, distinctive features, and dialect. Shimwali is spoken on Grande Comore and Mohéli, and Shinzwani is spoken on Anjouan. The dialects are distinct, making communication between the different groups difficult.

The islands of Mohéli and Mayotte have a greater concentration of African settlers, with Arabic characteristics less evident among the people.

Culture is structured around the Islamic traditions of dress, diet, and social interaction. Society is matriarchal, and homesteads belong to the women. Rituals of song and dance play an important role in Comorian culture.

SOCIOECONOMIC FACTORS

The islands of Comoros form one of the world's poorest nations, with few natural resources and no known mineral deposits. Deforestation and erosion have damaged the environment.

Even though less than half the land is suitable for farming, agriculture is the backbone of the economy. The vast majority of people support themselves through subsistence agriculture, with wage earners making up only 5 percent of the population. Rice is the staple crop, but total production only meets 10 percent of local food needs. The people cultivate vanilla, cloves and ylang-ylang as cash crops.

Population growth puts pressure on food provision, employment and infrastructure. The population is expected to reach 750,000 by the turn of the century. Two-thirds of the people are under the age of 25. Unemployment is high in urban areas, especially among young people. There are, however, positions open that require more training and skills, since many skilled Comorians leave the island to find employment in African countries, Madagascar or Europe.

Education

Under French rule, only 23 percent of children received an education. Since independence, Comorians have been training as teachers, and by 1982, 60 percent of primary school-age children were attending school. The government's goal is to provide an education for every child through Koranic schools.

Health

Malaria is endemic, affecting about 80 percent of the population. In 1980, the World Bank estimated that half of all Comorian children die before reaching the age of four.

Table 1: SOCIAL INDICATORS IN BRIEF

Total enrollment in education	75,776
% of enrollment in primary education	81%
% of enrollment in secondary education	18%
% of enrollment in tertiary education (mainly abroad)	1%
Literacy rate	60%
Population per hospital bed and health care centers	460
Population per physician	21,300
Population per nurse	2,769
Infant mortality rate (per 1000)	280
Population in the 0-14 age group	47%

RELIGION

Ninety-nine percent of the Comorian people are Muslim. About 1,400 mosques are scattered across the islands. Children between the ages of four and twelve attend Koranic schools, where they absorb Islamic values.

Islanders subscribe to Sunni Islamic beliefs, but customs and traditions are steeped in African tradition and superstition. For many, Islam is a veneer covering folk religion. This is particularly true in rural areas.

Those with Muslim parents are not permitted to change their faith and may be imprisoned for converting to Christianity. There are other costs of conversion in addition to legal penalties. Most of the people fear and respect their elder leaders, who teach Islamic religion and culture. They also fear reprisals from the spirit world if they do anything contrary to Islam. In this matriarchal society, women are especially resistant to Christianity, since they can be dispossessed if they accept it.

Christianity is seen as a western religion. Those who have been exposed to Christianity, either through Koranic schools, through visits or study overseas, or from watching Western tourists, frequently have negative impressions of the faith. Any formal evangelistic program would be offensive to the people and the government.

There is freedom, however, for Christians to speak to their friends and acquaintances about their faith. Although Comorians appear to be resistant to change, below the surface many seem to be seeking and questioning. A small number of Comorians have become Christians. These believers, who number about 80 to 100, gather informally in homes or outdoors. They meet with caution since the laws of the country forbid conversion to Christianity.

Those who are not born to Muslim parents are free to worship as they choose. Only 1 percent of Comorians, including expatriates, profess to be Christian. A small church on Grande Comore ministers to Malagasy people and expatriates. Comorians are not permitted to attend. There is a small nucleus of believers among the 30 to 50 people who attend services.

FOREIGN MISSIONARIES

Colonial settlers brought Catholicism to the islands but honored the request of the Islamic sultans and avoided evangelizing Muslims. The church has remained small and has mainly attracted expatriates.

Protestant witness began in 1973, when Chris Fourie, a Dutch Reformed minister from South Africa, visited Comoros and was moved by the needs of the people. During one of his visits, a young Comorian man converted to Christianity. Fourie approached Africa Inland Mission, requesting that they begin a ministry on the islands. After a number of survey trips, work on Grande Comore was established.

Since no organized evangelism programs are permitted, Africa Inland Mission (AIM) operates as the Voluntary Services Group on the islands of Grande Comore and Anjouan as well as Mayotte. Expatriates provide technical assistance to the Comorian people, and are involved in a wide variety of work ranging from medical services, education, veterinary care, teaching, and skills training. There are no expatriate workers on the island of Mohéli.

LITERATURE AND SCRIPTURE DISTRIBUTION

Although Arabic is taught in schools, most people were not able to read the Arabic New Testament when it was introduced. Comorians are used to reading French, since French is the language of commerce. French Scriptures are available.

AIM has one missionary working to translate Scripture into Shimaore, the dialect of Mayotte, and the New Testament will soon be available. Portions have been sent to the United Bible Society for publishing. Difficulties in translation work include a lack of orthographies.

The Shimaore translation of the Scripture is also understood by those living on the island of Anjouan. Translations into other dialects are being considered.

There is no duty on books imported into the country.

MAYOTTE

Mayotte was the first of the Comoros islands to be occupied by the French. In 1975 Comoros declared unilateral independence with the people of Mayotte voting against inclusion in the Islamic republic.

The island, with 376 Km^2 (145 sq miles) of land, is home to 67,167 people (Census 1985). This figure includes 2,500 expatriates. Most of the people speak Shimaore. Principal towns are Dzaoudzi, with a population of 5,865, and Mamoudzou, with a population of 12,026.

Mayotte is governed by a government commissioner and a general council consisting of 17 members. The president of the council is Younoussa Bamana.

The French franc is used as currency on the island. The economy is based on agriculture, but the people are not self-sufficient in food production.

In 1984, 15,000 children were registered in primary schools, and nearly 1,400 in secondary schools. The literacy rate is 63 percent. About 2,000 new job-seekers enter the labor market each year, but jobs are limited and few will find work.

There are two hospitals and seven doctors on the island. Elementary nursing training is available on the island. Nurses needing further training must go to Réunion or France.

The people of Mayotte are 98 percent Muslim and 2 percent Christian (mainly Roman Catholic). Although the majority are Muslim, French rule provides greater freedom of religion than in the rest of Comoros. Christians may openly present the gospel of Jesus Christ and there is no official penalty for conversion. Because Mayotte is an Islamic society, however, caution must be taken in any evangelistic endeavor.

Roman Catholics have a church on Mayotte with approximately 250 people attending, and about 2,000 to 3,000 adherents. Many are expatriates.

The International Protestant Church is the only Protestant church on the island, and its pastor is an AIM missionary. The congregation consists of about 60 people, including children. Mainly Malagasy people and expatriates attend, but ten local people have professed faith in Christ.

The church runs a Theological Education by Extension (TEE) program that disciples believers, and even trains some with only basic literacy skills. Members have opened a reading room to encourage people outside the church to come in and meet Christians.

In 1983, 13,800 radio receivers operated on Mayotte. The International Protestant Church broadcasts a 15-minute radio program each Sunday on the national radio service. This transmission is heard on the other islands as well. FEBA programs in French are also received.

Jehovah's Witnesses are working on Mayotte. Between 30 and 40 people attend their services.

NEEDS IN COMOROS AND MAYOTTE

- Prayer is requested for a breakdown of Satanic strongholds on the islands.
- Tentmaking missionaries are needed to serve the people of Comoros through medical care, education and practical training.
- There is a shortage of medical supplies, even though no import duties are levied on these items.
- Christian tourists need wisdom. Indiscriminate tract or Scripture distribution may create difficulties for local churches.
- Christians in difficult places like Comoros need prayer. Building relationships in this anti-Christian climate is hard work and often discouraging.

BIBLIOGRAPHY

Economist Intelligence Unit, *EIU Country Report No. 1*, 1990.

Economist Intelligence Unit, *Madagascar, Comores, Mauritius, Seychelles Country Report 1989/90*.

Europa Publications, *Africa South of the Sahara 1989*, Europa Publications.

World Bank, *The Comoros: Current Economic Situation and Prospects 1983*.

DEMOCRATIC REPUBLIC OF MADAGASCAR

Co-edited by Marc T. Rakoto

Profile

Natural features: A large island separated from the African continent by the Mozambique channel. Land area: 592,800 km^2 (228,880 square miles), extending 1,600 kilometers (1,000 miles) from north to south and more than 500 kilometers (390 miles) from east to west at the widest point. Mountainous central plateau running from north to south, with coastal plains. Highest point: Mount Tsaratanana at 2,800 m (9,200 feet).

Climate: Tropical, with cyclones as a common occurrence. Inland, the climate is temperate. Average temperatures range from 15°C (58°F) in July to 21°C (69°F) in January.

Population: 11.94 million (1990 estimate). Annual growth rate (1980 - 1985): 3.2%. Population density ranges from 30 per km^2 on the central plateau to 2 per km^2 on the west coast. Life expectancy: 53 years.

Ethnic groups: 98% Malagasy and 2% Asians, Comorians, and Westerners.

Languages and literacy: Malagasy and French are the official languages. Although there are 18 tribes with varying dialects, all of them understand Malagasy. Literacy is 53%, but the percentage of functionally literate is lower.

Government: One party state, with the President, Admiral Didier Ratsikara, held accountable by the Supreme Revolutionary Council. The People's National Assembly has some legislative functions. There are six provinces (*faritany*).

Urbanization: 21% (1985). The average annual growth rate was 5.3% between 1980 and 1985. Capital city is Antananarivo with a population of 1,250,000 (1988). There are six provincial capitals. Main towns are Mahajanga (200,000); Fianarantsoa (300,000); Antsiranana (220,000); and Antsirabe (100,000). Toamasina, with about 230,000 people, is the main port.

Economy: Currency: 100 centines = 1 Franc *malagache*. Average exchange rate for 1990: Mgfr 1500 = US $1. GDP: Mgfr 4,200 billion (1990). GDP per capita US $110 (1988). Inflation: 11% in 1990. Exports: US $350 million (1990). Imports: US$490 million. France is main trading partner. Inflation rate: 9% in 1990. Growth rate: 4.0% in 1990 (0.5% from 1960-1988). Agriculture as % of GDP: 31% in 1990; Industry; 15%. Labor force in agriculture: 75% in 1986.

Religion: Traditional, 47%; Roman Catholic, 26%; Protestant, 22%; Muslim, 2.7%; Indigenous churches, 2.2%; Anglican, 1.3%; Sects and non-Christian, 1%.

HISTORICAL BACKGROUND

According to oral tradition, the Vazimba people of San origin were the earliest inhabitants of Madagascar. Advancing immigrants drove them into the mountainous areas. Although the majority of the Vazimba have been absorbed into Malagasy society, pockets of people still call themselves Vazimba.

The Malagasy people are descendants of immigrants from Polynesia, Indonesia and Africa who arrived in successive waves. Indonesian immigration began in about the eighth century. Later, Arab, Chinese and Indian people arrived.

The Marina people have dominated the island since ancient times, when the society was a monarchy. A significant Marina monarch was Andrianampoinimerina, who established an efficient government. By 1850, his descendant tribe controlled most of Madagascar and continues to be the ruling ethnic group today.

The first European explorers reached Madagascar in the fifteenth century, but were pushed out repeatedly by the inhabitants. Eventually, Madagascar became a stopping point for navigators on their way to the east. Strong links with Britain developed in the eighteenth and nineteenth centuries, and trade and cultural links expanded. When the Suez Canal opened, the island was no longer as important to trade, and European interest diminished.

In 1896, Madagascar was annexed by France. The country was under French rule until its independence in 1960. In 1972, a group of dissident students led a succesful coup against the government of President Tsiranana.

In 1975, President Didier Ratsiraka was elected in a referendum to head the Supreme Revolutionary Council of the newly-constituted Democratic Republic of Madagascar. Socialist policies and state enterprises were introduced, and import and export trade was nationalized. An agreement with the International Monetary Fund in 1980 specified reforms that are still underway.

SOCIOECONOMIC CONDITIONS

The economy of Madagascar depends on agriculture, which accounts for 90 percent of its exports. Some 80 percent of its population live in rural areas, and 88 percent of the country's labor force are engaged in agriculture. Paddy rice is the main crop and the staple diet of the people. Even though the government is aiming at self-sufficiency in food, the production of rice is decreasing. Cash crops are coffee, which accounts for 40 percent of export earnings, cotton, cloves and vanilla. Falling coffee prices have negatively affected the economy.

Some 51 percent of the population are of working age (between 15 and 64). About 65 percent of the people live at subsistence level.

Madagascar's mountainous areas make communication difficult. Roads are generally poor and often impassable in the rainy season, but air travel is common.

Education

Education in Madagascar was started by Christian churches, and although there are a number of state schools, education is still largely in the hands of the church. Primary education is in Malagasy and secondary education is in French.

Primary school education is now compulsory for all children. Thirty-six percent of children within the appropriate age range attend secondary schools. An estimated 54,000 young people leave school each year, but only about 20,000 will find jobs.

Although the official literacy figure is 53 percent, the number of functionally literate is very low in rural areas.

Health

Malaria is endemic, even in the highlands. More than 20 percent of babies born in Madagascar die before the age of four. Traditional healers play a large part in rural health care. The government's goal is to provide accessible healthcare at the village level.

Table 1: SOCIAL INDICATORS IN BRIEF

Total enrollment in education	2,192,541
% enrolled in primary schools	72%
% enrolled in secondary schools	24%
% enrolled in tertiary education	4%
Adult literacy rate	53%
Population per doctor	10,180
Population per nurse	2,495
Infant mortality rate	109 per 1000

% under the age of 14	45%
Population growth rate (1980-85)	3.2%
Life expectancy	53 years

[1] *United Bible Society estimate*

THE PEOPLE

The Malagasy language reveals the Indonesian and Polynesian origins of the Malagasy people.

Later immigrants were Arab traders who settled in the north. Although they were originally Muslim, their practice of Islam was eventually absorbed into Malagasy folk religion.

Today the people in the north have Arab characteristics, while in the south, Creole people of African origin are in the majority.

Of the 18 Malagasy tribes, the largest is the Marina tribe, who most closely resemble their Indonesian and Malaysian forebearers. The Marina live mainly in the highland plateau and account for about 25 percent of the total population.

Prominent among the coastal tribes is the Betsimisarako, also known as the Cotiers, who comprise the second largest population group.

The Asian community retains its own distinctiveness and has not integrated into Malagasy society. Most Asians, including 16,000 Chinese, migrated to Madagascar during French rule and live along the eastern coastal towns.

There are about 17,000 Indians and Pakistanis in Madagascar. It is difficult to count this group since many of them carry dual passports. They work in small-scale commerce and are commonly known as Karana traders. The majority are Shi'ite Muslims. Some identify closely with Iranian revolutionaries.

Islam's influence in Madagascar is growing, and there is evidence of oil money financing Islamic missionary work.

Other non-Malagasy populations include 25,000 Comorians, 18,000 French, 4,000 people from Mauritius, and 22,000 from other countries including Lebanon, Syria, and a range of African and European nations.

STATUS OF CHRISTIANITY

A Jesuit, Luis Mariano, was the first missionary to visit Madagascar. Between 1613 and 1619, he journeyed around the island, but was unable to arouse any interest in his message. Lazarite Brothers arrived in 1657 during the French occupation, but were also unsuccessful.

London Missionary Society (LMS) missionaries arrived in Madagascar in 1818. Tragedy struck the group when five members of the two families died of malaria within six months of arrival, leaving the Rev. David Jones as the only survivor.

This devastating loss did not deter Jones. In 1920, he returned with James Hastie. They were favorably received by the king, and established a school for children of the royal household, the first of many schools in Madagascar. Their great concern was the slave trade, and within a short space of time persuaded King Radama I to stop this practice.

The Malagasy language was written for the first time in script other than Arabic, and the New Testament and later the Old Testament were translated.

Radama I died in 1828 and was succeeded by his widow Ranavalona I. Initially, she lifted a ban against the sacraments and Christian marriage, sparking a period of rapid church growth. Reactions against Christianity began, however, and a wave of persecution swept the country. Christians were burned, stoned or thrown off precipices. Many of them went to their death singing and praying. Rasalama was the first Christian martyr, and her name is still revered today. Other Christians fled, and Christianity spread across the island.

Christians met secretly to worship, and by the end of that period, the number of Christians had grown considerably. The persecution of Christians continued for twenty years until the death of Ranavalona I. She was succeeded by her son Radama II, who opened Madagascar's doors to foreign missionaries once again.

The long period of persecution had aroused international interest in Madagascar. After Radama II took over, Roman Catholic missionaries were the first to arrive in 1861. Missionaries with the London Missionary Society who had left during the persecution returned in 1862. Anglican workers arrived soon after in 1864.

In 1869, the Queen and her consort were baptized, and she ordered her idol and fetishes to be burned. Many people turned to God as a result.

Norwegian Lutherans began their work in 1867. American Quakers were other early entrants. Their work was later consolidated into the work of the Church of Jesus Christ in Madagascar (FJKM).

With the French takeover of the country in 1896, a second wave of persecution against the Protestant church started. Many church buildings were confiscated and schools closed.

Revival movements

A review of the growth of the church in Madagascar would be incomplete without mentioning the revival movements that have played a major role. In 1895, a man named Rainisoalambe from the south-central plateau preached the gospel, casting out demons and healing. His co-workers came to be known as "shepherds," and were drawn from all main Protestant denominations.

Later, three other movements took place in the country. The first took place in Manolotreny, near Soatanana. The second occurred in Farihimena from 1946 to 1948. The third movement was started in 1941 in the southeast of the island by a woman named Velahavana Germaine, who came to be known as Ankaramalaza.

Church leaders have acknowledged that these movements brought revival in the past, and that some are continuing to bring revival today. Churches consecrate shepherds after their training. Some of these trained workers have started indigenous churches.

The church today

Despite the costly beginnings of Christianity in Madagascar, both Roman Catholic and Protestant churches have struggled with nominalism and syncretism over the years. Many people identify strongly with their ancestors, and men especially have many responsibilities on behalf of the dead.

About two-thirds of church members are women. The number of evangelicals is estimated to number between 15 percent and 20 percent of those who claim to be Christian.

A new emphasis on spiritual warfare and release of those captive to the spirit world is bringing people back to church. The number of people who renounce syncretism is growing, mainly because of lay witness.

There is a need for unity, both between denominations as well as between churches and parachurch organizations. Problems arise when people converted through a parachurch ministry attend churches that offer only one service a week. These new converts feel the need for discipleship training. Christian agencies organize Bible studies during the week to meet this need, threatening some churches.

Table 2: ESTIMATED RELIGIOUS AFFILIATION

Traditional religion	47.0%
Roman Catholic	26.0%
Protestant	22.0%
Indigenous churches	2.2%
Muslim	2.2%
Anglican	1.3%
Sects and non-Christian	1.0%

Table 3: ESTIMATED CHURCH MEMBERSHIP IN MADAGASCAR

Roman Catholic Church	2,600,000
Church of Jesus Christ in Madagascar	1,500,000
Malagasy Lutheran Church	800,000
Anglican church	163,000
Seventh Day Adventist church	65,000
Pentecostal Church Jesus Saves	40,000
FSSM	35,000
Free Evangelical Church	24,000
Protestant Christian Church of Witness	19,000
Jesus Only	12,000
Bible Baptist Church of Madagascar (FBBM)	4,000
Assemblies of God	3,000

Smaller churches include:

- Biblical Baptist Church
- Evangelical Church of Tulear
- Free Evangelical Church
- Independent Evangelical Church
- L'Eglise Evangelique de Reveil
- L'Eglise Pentecostist Evangelique

NATIONAL CHURCHES

Roman Catholic Church

Although Roman Catholics tried to enter Madagascar in ear-lier years, it was not until after the death of Queen Ranavalona in 1861 that they resumed efforts to enter Madagascar.

In 1861, Jesuit priests arrived and received the blessing of Radama I. They began work among the Betsileo people. Through the introduction of schools, their work grew rapidly. Under French rule, the church expanded without any hindrances.

Today, the Roman Catholic Church (*Fiangona Katolika Apostolika Romanina or FKAR*) is the largest single church in Madagascar, with 2.6 million baptized members. The Lazarites work in the southern part of the country, and the Holy Ghost Fathers work in the northern part. While the organization of the church is in the hands of Malagasy archbishops and bishops, there are still more expatriate clergy than national clergy.

Roman Catholicism is stronger in the south among the Creole people. The church consists of three archdiocese and 14 diocese.

Anglican church

The persecution of Christians under Queen Ravanalona drew worldwide attention. When Madagascar was re-opened to missionaries, the Anglican church responded. In 1865, the Society for the Propagation of the Gospel (SPG) was the first Anglican agency to send clergy, followed by the Church Missionary Society, which later withdrew when the SPG appointed a bishop in 1874. The appointing of a bishop established the Malagasy Episcopal Church.

Anglican outreach to the community was through schools. The educational program as well as church growth suffered under French rule because classes had to be taught in French.

The church saw training Malagasy priests as a priority. A theological college and two training colleges for catechists were established. By 1961, only two of 61 priests were expatriates.

Today the Anglican Church in Madagascar (*Fiangonana Episkopaly eto Madagasikara*) forms part of the Church of the Province of the Indian Ocean and embraces the Malagasy Episcopal Church of earlier years. Three dioceses care for an estimated 163,000 adherents.

Protestant churches

The Protestant church in Madagascar consists of two groups— large denominations with origins in early missionary work, and smaller groups with more recent origins.

An early agreement between the two main denominations resulted in the Reformed church (FJKM) working in the north, and the Lutheran church in the south. This agreement became difficult to maintain when people moved from their home areas, and it has largely fallen away.

Two main church associations draw the major denominations together. The Christian Council of Churches in Madagascar or *Fiombonan'ny Fiangonana Kristiana Eto Madagascar* (FFKM) has the following members:

- Malagasy Lutheran Church (FLM)
- Roman Catholics
- Anglican church (FLM)
- Church of Jesus Christ in
  Madagascar (FJKM)

The Federation of Protestant Churches in Madagascar, also known as *Fiombanan'ny Fiangonana Protestanta Eto Madagasikara* (FFPM), is made up of the Church of Jesus Christ in Madagascar (FJKM) and the Malagasy Lutheran Church.

CHURCH OF JESUS CHRIST IN MADAGASCAR
(FIANGONAN'I JESOA KRISTY ETO MADAGASIKARA OR FJKM)

After many years of negotiating, this church formed out of a union between work done by the London Missionary Society, the Paris Missionary Society and the Friends Foreign Missionary Association. It is now the largest Protestant church in Madagascar.

Missionaries of the London Missionary Society arrived in 1818 and soon began to play an important role in the development of the country. Schools were established and artisan missionaries became involved in projects at the request of the monarch. Churches grew rapidly, and by 1870, there were 260 churches with 20,000 communicant members.

French colonial rule brought difficult times for the Protestant church. Churches and schools were taken over. The Paris Missionary Society, less threatening to the French than an English mission, came in to help.

Today the church functions through a national synod, divided into 77 regional synods. About 1,000 pastors minister in 3,000 congregations. Most are in the northern part of the country. FJKM churches have three seminaries and a theological faculty. There are about 1.5 million church members.

Church members have been at the forefront of social development in Madagascar. Many schools are under the church's care, as well as a number of agricultural development projects.

Churches have a renewed focus on personal Christian growth and discipleship.

LUTHERAN CHURCH OF MADAGASCAR
(FIANGONANA LOTERANA ETO MADAGASIKARA)

Lutheran witness began in 1867, when the first Norwegian Lutheran Mission workers arrived. They strongly emphasized the provision of schools and medical work. One of their earliest missionaries was a medical doctor, Dr. C. Borchgrevink, who was greatly loved by the people. Twenty years later, they were joined by American Lutherans, who were followed by Danish Lutherans.

In 1950, the Malagasy Lutheran Church was formed, combining the work of the different Lutheran missions under indigenous leadership.

In the 70s an evangelism-in-depth program was established, mobilizing the church, and bringing revival and church growth. Growth and revival continues through a ministry called "shepherds" evangelism, operating in all the main protestant groups.

Training local leaders has played an important role in the development of the church. A training institute was established in 1871, and 100 years later, 1,000 Lutheran pastors had graduated from the institute. Today, a seminary at Fianarantsoa trains candidates for the ministry. Six Bible institutes train evangelists.

The Lutheran church now has a multi-faceted ministry. Ten synods serve approximately 800,000 church members and adherents. The medical arm of the mission, known as SALFA, provides village health programs, four hospitals with many dispensaries and two leprosy centers. The Lutheran education program has 80,000 children in 90 primary schools and 35 secondary schools. Teachers are trained at nine centers. There are two schools each for the deaf and blind, the only ones of their kind in the country. The church is assisted in this extensive social work by about 85 expatriate missionaries.

MALAGASY BAPTIST CHURCH

Malagasy Baptist Church developed from the ministry of the Conservative Baptist Foreign Mission. The mission's involvement in literature brought together groups of students who became the nuclei of new churches. A Bible training center has now been established to provide basic development training. Six missionaries assist in the ministry of this church.

ASSEMBLIES OF GOD
(FIANGONAN' ANDRI'AMANITRA)

Assemblies of God churches have been planted mainly in towns. New churches are established through the development of home groups. A Bible school in Antananarivo trains pastors for the ministry. The denomination had 3,000 members in 1985.

THE PENTECOSTAL CHURCH JESUS SAVES

The Pentecostal Church Jesus Saves started in 1963 and has grown rapidly. Today they have 200 churches. Members have started schools and run a Bible school in Antananarivo.

Pentecostal churches are multiplying, but to some extent at the cost of mainline churches. A probable reason for their growth is an emphasis on power encounters with evil forces.

FOREIGN MISSIONARIES

About 120 expatriate missionaries work in Madagascar.

The Norwegian Missionary Society has the largest number of missionaries there. A staff of about 60 missionaries is involved mainly in medical and development work. The Evangelical Lutheran Church in America sends 27 missionaries to add to the number of Lutheran missionaries in Madagascar.

The Conservative Baptist Foreign Mission has been working in Madagascar since 1966 and now has six missionaries there. The

United Pentecostal Church International has sent eight missionaries to Madagascar to work with the national church.

Several evangelical mission groups started work in Madagascar in recent years. These include:

- *Southern Baptist Convention Foreign Mission Board*, which first sent missionaries to Madagascar in 1986, currently has two missionaries assisting the Bible Baptist Church of Madagascar in church planting;
- *Africa Inland Mission*, which has sent missionaries to Madagascar since 1980, supports existing ministries such as an agricultural program; and
- *Africa Evangelical Fellowship*, whose missionaries are recent arrivals, and have been invited to assist in the ministries of *Groupe Biblique des Travailleurs* (GBT).

UNREACHED PEOPLES

The majority of unreached people live in rural villages, including the Sakalava people in the north, the Tanala people in the southeast, the Mikea people on the west coast, and the Antankarana people.

Muslims in Madagascar are totally unreached and are comprised of a number of different groups:

- The *Antaimoro* are a distinct group whose roots go back to the thirteenth century, when Arab traders settled in the southeast of the country. They hold to some Muslim customs but are mainly animistic.
- Christians have a unique opportunity to reach Muslim *Comorians* living in Madagascar, since there are severe restrictions against conversion and Christian witness in Comoros.
- *Indian and Pakistani Muslims* are highly resistant to the gospel and will require a different approach than Malagasy Muslims.
- Pockets of *Syrian and Lebanese Muslims* live mainly around Mahajanga and Antananarivo.

A post-Lausanne II committee is coordinating a five-year national evangelization program.

CHRISTIAN ACTIVITIES

Evangelism

Evangelism is taking place both in the local churches and through parachurch organizations. "Shepherds" associated with the revival movement move into rural villages, healing people and performing exorcisms. They develop home groups that later grow into churches.

Members of *Groupe Biblique des Travailleurs* minister to professionals and workers through Bible study groups. They organize mass evangelism rallies, and also reach out to the needy through social action.

Several groups work among students and young people, including:

- Scripture Union, with work among children and young people, a conference center, camps, children's missions, literature distribution, and counseling to families;
- Youth and the Bible, a Pentecostal youth movement;
- Gospel Bible Union (UGBM), associated with Intervarsity Fellowship, working among students;
- Athletes in Action;
- *Centre Evangelisation de la Masse et des Intellectuels* (CEMI); and
- AVOTRA (YWAM), a ministry which works with churches in evangelism to children and to the poor and needy.

Broadcasting

With more than two million radios and 100,000 television sets in Madagascar, media resources are powerful tools for Christian ministry, both in evangelism and training.

The state-controlled Radio-Television Malagasy permits Christian broadcasts, and doors are wide open for Christians to produce programs for the national service. FEBA, operating from Seychelles, transmits 28 hours of programs a month. FEBA programs are easily picked up and many people listen to them.

Trans World Radio (TWR), transmitting from Swaziland, beams two weekly programs in Malagasy. Programs are prepared in Europe by Malagasy students. TWR reports that responses to their programs reveal a need to increase broadcasts.

Other agencies involved in radio ministry include the Malagasy Lutheran Church, which has a recording studio; the Malagasy Bible Society; and Association Avotra.

Because of the low literacy rate, Malagasy Bible Society and PRM International provide a limited number of New Testaments on tape.

Literature

Many churches and para-church agencies are involved in the production and distribution of Christian literature.

Emmaus Bible correspondence courses enroll about 8,000 people, and play an important role in literature distribution.

Scripture Gift Mission produces literature in Malagasy for distribution.

The Conservative Baptist Church has a literature ministry known as *Edisiona Vaovao Mahafaly,* which includes a bookstore and a printing department at Antananarivo. An extensive correspondence course ministry has resulted in the formation of several new churches.

The Malagasy Lutheran Church has a large commercial print shop.

Scripture Union is active in literature ministry through the distribution of daily reading notes and a bookshop that provides an outlet for Christian literature.

A number of Christian magazines, journals, and newssheets are published regularly. These include:

- The Roman Catholic Church's
  Lakroan'i Madagasikara
- FJKM's *Vaovao FJKM* and *Mpanolotsaina*
- The Lutheran church's
  Ny Sakaizan'Ny Tanora
- Pentecostal Church Jesus Saves'
  bimonthly magazine
- *Iksa Mianakavy,* a journal on
  Christian family life
- *Toriteny Sy Fampianarana,*
  a Protestant journal
- *Ny Fampiononana,* a religious review
- *Fiaraha Mivavaka Tsan'adro,* a quarterly
  Protestant publication
- *Iafan 'Iarivo,* a quarterly Catholic journal
- *Mpamangy,* a Lutheran journal on
  religion and culture
- *Ny Fiainana Ao Amin'i Kristy*
- *Fiaraha Mivavaka Tsan'Adro*

Scripture distribution

The Malagasy Bible was the first complete Bible published in Africa. It was printed in 1835 on a hand press in Tananarive. Missionaries hastened to distribute copies and it was released just as the reign of terror began. Copies were buried or hidden in caves to save them from being burned.

The 150th anniversary of the first Bible's publication was a cause for great celebration and special souvenir editions of the Bible increased sales.

A new translation of the New Testament in Malagasy has been completed and is being distributed.

The Malagasy Bible Society sold or distributed 41,595 Bibles in 1987, 56,571 New Testaments, and nearly 800,000 portions or selections of Scripture. Many bookshops across the country sell Scriptures.

Christian education

Early missionaries entering Madagascar recognized the need to train Christians for ministry. The London Missionary Society, the Anglican missions and the Lutheran missions all established training centers to train ministers and evangelists. Today, there are many seminaries and colleges in Madagascar.

Smaller evangelical and Pentecostal groups see the need for Biblically-based training, and a number of new colleges have opened in recent years.

The Church of Jesus Christ in Madagascar has four theological colleges at Ivato, Ambatonakanga, Mandritsara, and Amboniavaratra (Fianarantsoa).

The Malagasy Lutheran Church has a theological seminary at Fianarantsoa that offers a five-year diploma, a regional theological college at Betioky-Atsimo, and five colleges for pastoral training.

The Anglican church has a theological college at Antananarivo that offers a four year Diploma in Theology training. Two pastoral colleges train catechists.

The School of the Prophets, the training college of the Malagasy Protestant Church, is in Antananarivo.

The Assemblies of God in Madagascar has a Biblical college in Antananarivo.

The Malagasy Baptist Church has a Bible school at Antsirabe. In addition, they continue to be involved in Theological Education by Extension (TEE).

Pentecostal Church Jesus Saves has a Bible school at Antananarivo. Students are trained for three years, take two years of practical work and then return for a further year of study.

The revival movement within the Protestant federation uses about 50 revival centers spread across the island to train shepherds. Many needy people are cared for at these centers.

Social concerns

The first task of the London Missionary Society when missionaries arrived in Madagascar in the early nineteenth century was to establish a school. This was the beginning of a social action program that has been part of the history of the church throughout the years.

The Malagasy Lutheran Church runs extensive medical and educational programs that include three hospitals, two leprosaria and many dispensaries and health care centers.

Education programs are the main activity of the Church of Jesus Christ in Madagascar, with 180 primary schools and 54 secondary schools. Agricultural and development schemes operate in a number of areas.

The Malagasy Bible Society has been involved in an agricultural scheme and an adult literacy program.

Fikrifama (Christian Rural Development and Water Resources Program) is a water development project run jointly by four church groups.

Groupe Biblique des Travailleurs serves the poor and needy.

NEEDS IN MADAGASCAR

- Pastors are motivated to evangelize the country, but desire more training.

- Many groups of people have never heard of Christ's salvation in a meaningful way. They live in villages along inaccessible coastal areas. Few churches or para-church groups have goals to reach Asian Muslims and the Chinese peoples. National Christian leaders are calling for a coordinated strategy to evangelize all of Madagascar.

- Christians in Madagascar want Christian literature, particularly in Malagasy.

BIBLIOGRAPHY

Brown, Mervyn, *Madagascar Rediscovered*, Damien Tunnacliffe, 1978.

Econonomist Quarterly Indicators: First Quarter 1991.

EIU Country Profile 1990/91.

Europa Publications, *Africa South of the Sahara 1989.*

Gove, Max and Houriet Maurice, *Survey of Madagascar.*

Gow, Bonar A., *Madagascar and the Protestant Impact*, Longman 1979.

Halverson, Alton C.O., *Madagascar: Footprints in the Sand*, Augsburg Publishing House, 1973.

McMahon, E.O., *Christian Missions in Madagascar*, SPG 1914.

Rajoelina, P. and Ramelet Alain, *Madagascar: la Grande Ile*, L'Harmattan, 1989.

United Bible Society, *World Annual Reports*, 1987, 1988, 1989.

United Nations Fund for Population Development, *Population Policy Compendium, Madagascar.*

US Department of State, *Background Notes*, Sept. 1984.

REPUBLIC OF MALAWI

Co-edited by Willie Musopole

Profile

Natural features: Landlocked country sharing borders with Zambia, Mozambique and Tanzania. 118,484 km^2 (45,747 square miles) of land area. Malawi is a long narrow country, some 840 km from north to south, varying in width from 80 to 160 km (50 to 100 miles). Plateau country dominated by Lake Malawi at 23,310 km^2 (9,000 square miles). Altitudes range from 900 m – 1200 m (3,000 feet-4,000 feet) on the plateau, to Mulanje mountain with an altitude of 3000 m (10,000 feet).

Climate: May to August is cool and dry with temperatures ranging from 12-22°C (54-72°F). September to November is hot and dry with an average maximum temperature of 29°C (85°F). November to April is hot with rainfall varying from 700 to 1800 mm a year (28-72 inches).

Population: 8,550,000 (mid-1990 estimate). Annual growth rate: 3.5% (est. 1987). Population density: 82 per km^2.

Ethnic groups: Six major ethnic groups: Chewa, Tumbuka, Tonga, Lomwe, Yao, and Ngoni.

Languages and literacy: Official languages: English and Chichewa. Literacy rate: 59% (UNESCO 1985). Functionally literate: 27% (1987).

Urbanization: 13% (1987). Urban centers: Lilongwe (capital) population 223,000; Blantyre 332,000.

Government: One-party republic with a presidential form of government. Life president: Dr. Hastings Kamuza Banda, in whom executive powers are vested. Parliament: National Assembly headed by president.

Economy: Currency: 100 Tambala = 1 Malawi Kwacha; MK2.716= US$1 (average for 1990). GDP (1988): K3699 million. GDP per capita (1989): K477 (US$167). Growth rate (1990): 6%. Inflation rate (1990): 15%. Imports (1990): US$590m. Exports: US$330m. Employment in Agriculture: 85% of population. Agriculture as % of GDP; 35% (1989), 90% of exports.

Religion: Protestant 34%, Roman Catholic 26%, African Independent 19%, Anglican 1%, Muslim 15%, Traditional 5%.

HISTORICAL BACKGROUND

Early inhabitants of Malawi were hunter-gatherer people of
Bushmen (San, Basarwa) and pygmy origin. From the twelfth century, Malawi was settled by Bantu groups. The largest group was
the Maravi people, made up of a number of sub-groups. The
Chewa sub-group was numerically the largest, and Chichewa has
now become the main language of the Maravi people.

Northern Malawi was settled by the Tumbuka and Tonga peoples. Later arrivals were the Lomwe and Yao from Mozambique,
and the Ngoni people from the south.

Malawians suffered the horrors of the slave trade, and for
some years, up to 10,000 slaves were transported to the coast annually even though missionaries like David Livingstone worked
towards its abolition.

In 1881, Britain proclaimed that the area was a British protectorate, naming it Nyasaland Districts Protectorate (Nyasaland
Protectorate in 1907). Administration was through indirect rule
that permitted tribal administration.

In 1953, when the Central African Federation was formed to
create a union between Nyasaland and the two Rhodesias, there
was considerable resistance within Nyasaland. In 1962, Britain accepted Nyasaland's withdrawal. Independence was gained in
1964, and the country's name was changed to Malawi under the
leadership of a moderate, Dr. Kamuzu Hastings Banda. Today,
President Banda is aging and succession has become a dominant
topic in political discussion, but the national political situation is
calm.

SOCIOECONOMIC CONDITIONS

Malawi is a poor country with limited land and high population density. It is landlocked, and rail outlets to the coast through
war-torn Mozambique have been closed, leaving Malawi no alter-
native but the costly 4,000 km routes through South African ports.
Rail services have resumed through Mozambique, but this route is
tenuous as long as civil war in that country continues. Tea and tobacco industries, which provide about 70 percent of foreign exchange earnings, have been heavily hit.

Despite all of this, Malawi, with its free enterprise economy,
has become one of Africa's success stories. Between 1970 and 1980,
Malawi had a higher economic growth rate than any other central
African country. Over this period, food production rose by a stag-

gering 30 percent. Low urban wages helped to keep people out of the towns and on their lands, and also helped to keep the price of manufactured goods competitive with imported goods. The average wage for all Malawians was K87.3 ($34) in 1988.

Table 1: SOCIAL INDICATORS IN BRIEF

Total enrollment in education (1988/89)	1,203,000
% enrolled in primary schools	97%
% enrolled in secondary schools	2.3%
% enrolled in tertiary education	0.4%
Pupil/teacher ratio (1988/89)	65:1
Adult literacy rate	59%
No. of hospitals and health posts	750
Population per hospital bed (1986)	595
Population per doctor	42,236
Population per nurse	4,906
Infant mortality rate per 1,000 (1987)	150
Population in 0-14 age group	47%
Population growth rate (1988)	3.5% a year
Life expectancy at birth (1987)	48 years

Agriculture

Malawi is dependent on export crops for economic survival. Agriculture provides a living for 85 percent of the population. Some 56 percent of the land is arable. Major export crops are tobacco, tea, groundnuts and sugar. Malawi is one of the few countries in Africa that is able to feed itself. Maize is the principal food crop, but sorghum, millet and cassava are also grown. Although the people are poor, most have food to eat.

Education

In 1986, 48 percent of children eligible for primary school attended school. Current education policy aims to increase school attendance and improve the teacher/pupil ratio. Secondary education in Malawi began only in 1940, and today the country has one of the lowest enrollments in tertiary education in the region. There are five technical colleges, five teacher training colleges and a university. A medical faculty is being established at the University of Malawi.

Health

The general health status is poor and malaria is endemic. Health programs are gradually moving away from curative service, which was emphasized at independence, to health care with community participation. Of the 64 hospitals throughout the country, 20 are operated by church organizations.

The population growth rate is high. Women bear an average of 6.7 children each. The infant mortality rate is 150 per 1,000 live births, but UNICEF estimates that one-third of all children die before the age of five. According to a report by the Minister of Health to the World Health Organization, Malawi has 3,000 cases of AIDS. A public awareness campaign is gathering momentum.

Mozambican refugees

About 800,000 refugees now reside in Malawi. In the Nsanje district, about 260,000 refugees make up 60 percent of the total population in the district. Because the areas they come from are still unstable, attempts to repatriate these refugees are not progressing.

STATUS OF CHRISTIANITY

Historical review

David Livingstone, who is considered the father of missions in Malawi, explored the country thoroughly. When he returned to Scotland, his drive and enthusiasm spawned three missionary societies.

The first of these societies to send missionaries was the Universities' Mission to Central Africa. Livingstone, accompanied by Bishop Charles Mackenzie and a party of six, landed on the southern shore of Lake Malawi in 1861. Their first mission ended in failure. The place they had chosen for their work was on the slave route to the coast, and their opposition to the slave trade resulted in the enmity of the slave traders. Ultimately, Bishop Mackenzie contracted malaria and died. After only 15 months the party withdrew.

In 1874, the Free Church of Scotland established the Livingstonia Mission. Missionaries sent by this society also experienced hard times. After five years of ministry, there was only one convert and five missionary graves. The Church of Scotland, following shortly after, began in what is now Blantyre, naming the settlement after Livingstone's birthplace.

Other early entrants into Malawi were the Dutch Reformed Church from South Africa (1888), another group from the Universities' Mission to Central Africa, who started work in a different area in 1881, and the Seventh Day Adventist church.

No Malawi mission history would be complete without mentioning Joseph Booth, who has been described as a "religious hitchhiker." Booth first arrived in Malawi in 1892 when he requested land to start the Zambezi Mission of Baptist Theology and Practice. When he eventually was dismissed by the Zambezi Mission, he began the Nyasa Industrial Mission. He broke connections with this group as well, and began a third industrial mission called the Baptist Industrial Mission. Next, he worked with the Seventh Day Adventist church, taking over the Seventh Day Baptist Church (Plainsfield). A dispute arose and he left to start the Seventh Day Baptist Church (Central African Conference). Booth changed his allegiance again and helped establish the Watch Tower Society. He played an important role in the life of John Chilembwe, who started the Providence Industrial Mission (later banned following an uprising). His influence also resulted in the establishment of several Ethiopian-type independent churches.

Christianity today

Since the entrance of Christianity more than a century ago, churches have grown rapidly. The church with the largest affiliation is the Roman Catholic Church, with an estimated two million members. Of the Protestant denominations, the Church of Central Africa Presbyterian is by far the largest both numerically and in influence, with its membership approaching half a million.

There is freedom of religion for the propagation of the gospel and the establishment of the church. The government is sympathetic towards missionary work and allows the teaching of Scripture in the schools.

A large number of evangelistic crusades have been held in Malawi in recent years, awakening the church to its responsibility to reach the lost. They have also increased the willingness of different denominations to work together.

While a substantial number of Malawians attend church regularly, some see it as a part of becoming modernized and have little commitment to the teachings of the Bible. Christian leaders see reaching nominal Christians as a priority need.

The majority of church attendees are women. Programs aimed specifically at reaching men are limited.

Through movements such as the Students Christian Organization, many young people have gained a new understanding of Christianity but express frustration with the formality of mainline churches. As a result, small fellowship groups have mushroomed.

A large number of African Independent churches mix Christianity and traditional religion in varying degrees. Even in mainline churches, some people turn back to traditional religion in times of crisis. Jehovah's Witnesses show signs of revival in the border areas across from Zambia.

UNREACHED PEOPLES

Groups of people live in isolated areas without any exposure to the gospel of Jesus Christ.

Yao Muslims

The Yao people number approximately 900,000. About 90 percent are Muslims. Their Islamic tradition goes back to the pre-European era when the Yao were involved in the Arab slave trade, and their beliefs are an Africanized form of Islam. A new wave of Islamic fervor supported by countries in the Middle East is mounting, inspiring an aggressive campaign to turn Malawi into a Muslim state.

Mosques built at approximately 20 kilometer intervals have been financed by the Africa Muslim Agency, a Kuwait-based body. To date, over 50 major mosques and a hundred smaller mosques have been built. Several major Islamic centers have already been built and many more are under construction.

Hundreds of young men were sent to Kuwait for religious training before the 1991 Persian Gulf War. They are now back in Malawi, trying to spread their beliefs. Many Malawians from other language groups are accepting Islam.

Over the past few years, Malawians and expatriate missionaries have begun to respond to the needs of this previously neglected people group.

Asians

Asians numbered over 11,000 in the 1966 census. This figure shrank to 5,700 in the 1977 census. The Hindu community has a temple in Blantyre. At one time there were as many as 5,000 Hindus in Malawi. This figure is now estimated to be 1,100. Hinduism has not penetrated the black community.

Indian Muslims

The number of Indian Muslims has also declined. Most live in cities, and work in the professions, commerce, or trade.

Other groups

Most of the 800,000 refugees from Mozambique living in Malawi have never heard the good news of Jesus Christ. A small number of Sikhs live in Malawi. Baha'is are active in 991 localities in Malawi.

NATIONAL CHURCHES

The first church that began in Malawi was the Presbyterian church, and it grew rapidly. In 1902, the Roman Catholic Church was introduced and changed the scene. A report of a missionary conference in 1910 noted 17,511 Catholic members compared to 15,870 Presbyterians.

Early missionary societies emphasized the need to train Malawian pastors and leaders. Nationals took over the responsibility for their churches many years ago. The largest Protestant denomination, the Church of Central Africa Presbyterian, became an autonomous and indigenous church in 1958.

Many denominations and church groups operate in Malawi. About 30 have separated from denominational or mission churches. One hundred and twenty African Independent churches are scattered across Malawi.

Table 2: ESTIMATED RELIGIOUS AFFILIATION

Roman Catholic Church	34%
Protestant churches [1]	26%
African Independent churches[1]	19%
Muslim	15%
Traditional	5%
Anglican church	1%

[1] *Includes children of church-going parents.*

Churches may be grouped under two umbrella bodies:

The Christian Council of Malawi: Founded in 1939, this body has 13 member denominations and seven organizations. Its main activities are the Christian Services Committee, responsible for social activity; the Private Hospital Association of Malawi, which brings Christian medical work together; and a group that coordinates the churches' educational institutions.

The Evangelical Fellowship of Malawi: This body coordinates the efforts of evangelicals through a number of ministries. It sponsors New Life for All, an evangelistic outreach; Keswick conventions, an annual teaching ministry; pastors' conferences; and management and family seminars. The Evangelical Fellowship of Malawi is a member of the Association of Evangelicals of Africa and Madagascar.

Table 3: ESTIMATED RELIGIOUS AFFILIATION
OF THE LARGER DENOMINATIONS

Roman Catholic Church	2,000,000
Church of Central Africa Presbyterian	413,191
Anglican church	80,000
Seventh Day Adventist church	57,000
Church of Christ	50,000
National Baptist Convention	40,000

Baptist Mission in Malawi	38,000
Assemblies of God churches	30,000
Independent Baptist Convention	29,000
African Methodist Episcopal	18,000
Lutheran Church of Central Africa	14,500
Apostolic Faith Mission	7,500
Living Waters	7,000
Church of the Nazarene	6,700
Africa Evangelical Church	6,000
Free Methodist Church	6,000
Pentecostal Holiness Church	5,034
Evangelical Baptist Church	5,000
Seventh Day Baptist Church	4,500
Zambezi Evangelical Church	4,000
Free Baptist Church in Malawi	3,824
Faith Bible Ministries	3,500
Full Gospel Church	2,500

Roman Catholic Church

Although the Portuguese passed through Malawi many years before David Livingstone began his explorations, they made no attempt to establish any religious work. It was only in 1902, when the White Fathers and Montford Marist Fathers arrived, that Catholic educational centers were opened and churches established. Five years later, a group of converts was baptized. The work grew rapidly, and they planned a chain of stations across Malawi. In 1908, the Prefecture was raised to the status of Vicariate Apostolic.

A strong emphasis on a national church emerged. A seminary was started in 1912, and by 1929, the first Malawian nuns had taken their vows. The first Malawian priest, Cornelius Chitsulo, was ordained in 1937. In 1957, he became the first bishop. By 1970, there were 70 Malawian-born priests. Today, there are more than 400, 150 of whom are involved in secular ministry. More than 600 sisters work throughout Malawi.

The hierarchy consists of six diocese and the Archdiocese of Blantyre, where the Apostolic Nunciature is situated. The Catholic church's estimated two million adherents represent more than a quarter of Malawi's total population. The church serves the people of Malawi through 27 hospitals and health care units and 24 schools.

Anglican church (Church of the Province of Central Africa)

Missionaries sent by the Universities' Mission to Central Africa withdrew to Zanzibar following their failure to establish a mission in 1861.

William Johnson re-established this work in 1881, and decided to use the lake as the site to begin. He brought parts in 380 packages to build a small steamer, and the "Charles Janson" served the mission for 50 years. Headquarters were on Likoma Island. The area where missionaries began work was along the Islamic lakeshore, and the first priest to be ordained was a Yao, Yohama Abdulla, in 1898. Many schools were established along the lakeside and to the east and west of the lake, and in 1899, a college was established to train teachers. Education had a strong evangelical emphasis.

In 1909, Leonard Kamungu was ordained, and later pioneered work in eastern Zambia as possibly the first Malawian missionary. Today, the Anglican church, consisting of two diocese, has an estimated membership of 66,000 served by nearly 100 ministers. Only six ministers are expatriates. The Anglican church has three hospitals and nine health care centers under its care as well as primary and secondary schools.

Protestant churches

CHURCH OF CENTRAL AFRICA PRESBYTERIAN (CCAP)

This denomination is composed of three synods, each of which is autonomous in matters of administration and each with its own historical background. Discussion between these missions resulted in the formation of the Church of Central Africa Presbyterian in 1924, incorporating the Livingstonia and Blantyre Synods. The Nkhoma synod joined in 1926.

The roots of the Livingstonia mission date back to 1876, when the Free Church of Scotland sent a party of six men headed by Captain E.D. Young to start a mission in the Lake Malawi region. Included in the party was Dr. Robert Laws, a medical missionary. Over a period of 52 years, Dr. Laws played a leading role in establishing the mission, and later the church.

In 1877, the team was further strengthened by Dr. James Stewart and four evangelists from the Lovedale Institute in South Africa. One of the evangelists was William Koyi, who played an important role in establishing a mission among the Ngoni people. Work began at Cape Maclear, but was later moved to Bandawe.

In 1894, a revival broke out at their Khondowe mission station and thousands turned to Christ. Formal organization of an indigenous church began, and in 1899, the first presbytery of the Presbyterian Church of Central Africa was formed. The first Malawian was ordained in 1914.

The church emphasized social upliftment, and education programs, medical work, and industrial work developed beside evangelism programs.

By the year 1905, 30 years after missionaries arrived in the country, 10,000 converts worshiped at more than 350 preaching stations. Growth in this synod peaked in 1945 when the church membership of 34,143 constituted 1.6 percent of the total population. Despite steady growth, the percentage of membership in relation to the total population dropped to 1 percent by 1987 (69,000 members).

The Blantyre Synod began when Henry Henderson arrived in the country with the Livingstonia group but decided to travel south to establish a station in the Shire Highlands. He and Tom Bokwito, an African evangelist, secured a site and named it Blantyre. The mission struggled at first, and it was not until a new beginning was made in 1881 by the Reverend David Scott that a church was established. When Scott retired after 18 years of ministry, he had laid solid foundations for the establishment of an indigenous church.

The Reverend Harry Matecheta was the first national to be ordained, and subsequently became the first moderator of the Synod in 1939. Despite early difficulties, this church has grown rapidly and membership now totals 180,000. Church membership has risen from 1.5 percent of the total population in 1945 to a current 2.6 percent of total population. Only 40 ministers serve the 170 congregations scattered across the southern part of the country.

The Nkhoma Synod was started by the Dutch Reformed Church of South Africa. Missionaries set up the church's first mission station in 1889 at Mvere in the center of the country, with Livingstonia mission to the north and Blantyre synod to the south. Schools were started and a small medical work established, but the prime task of the church was seen to be evangelization.

In 1896, the headquarters of the mission was moved to Nkhoma, which developed into an extensive mission station with a hospital, schools, theological college, printing press, and workshops.

This synod has grown rapidly. It now has a membership of 164,000. There is a shortage of ministers, with 21 serving 89 congregations, and only a few more studying for ordination.

INDUSTRIAL MISSIONS

Towards the end of the last century, a number of industrial missions were started. They attempted to establish self-supporting ministries using non-ordained men who taught the people industrial skills. Joseph Booth was involved in the beginnings of Zambezi Industrial Mission, Nyasa Industrial Mission, and Baptist Industrial Mission.

The first of these was the Zambezi Industrial Mission, started by British Baptists in 1892. Eighteen years later, 35,000 people were hearing the gospel each month. Christian workers had established three hospitals and 5,000 were attending their schools. The work grew to form the Zambezi Evangelical Church, which became a synod of the United Evangelical Church in 1977.

Nyasa Industrial Mission began as an enterprise of the Australian Baptists in 1883. It is now the Ntambanyama synod of the United Evangelical Church.

Providence Industrial Mission, yet another industrial mission, was started in 1900 by John Chilembwe. This was a completely indigenous enterprise, although Chilembwe was influenced by Joseph Booth. In 1915, Chilembwe led an uprising that was quelled by the colonial administration, and he and a number of his followers were killed. The mission was banned, but later reopened. The National Baptist Assembly developed from this work.

CHURCH OF CHRIST

Church of Christ was introduced into Malawi in 1909 by a Malawian, Elaton Kundago, who had come under its influence while working in South Africa. The work was later strengthened by British missionaries. It was banned during the Chilembwe uprising, but the ban was later rescinded. This group of churches with about 50,000 members has seen a number of divisions and secessions.

SEVENTH DAY ADVENTISTS

Seventh Day Adventist work was started in 1902 by British missionaries. Their work grew steadily, and today they have over 57,000 members. There is a strong emphasis on social work, with two hospitals, a medical college, a leprosy control project, and five secondary schools. Dental clinics are at Blantyre and Lilongwe.

African independent churches

Around the turn of the century, a number of indigenous churches started forming. In some cases, there was a need to address the cultural issues facing the people, which were not being addressed in mission churches. For example, polygamy and beer-drinking were not addressed or were forbidden without discussion in mission churches. This lack of discussion created discontent. There was also failure on the part of missionaries to hand over responsibility to national Christians, which led to a break in trust between Malawians and expatriates.

Some of these indigenous groups are theologically close to mainline churches, while others are syncretistic or even non-Christian in belief. There are approximately 150 of these churches and they are growing quickly. About 19 percent of the population belong to one of these churches. Some leaders of these churches are calling for an umbrella body to coordinate their efforts and give them a voice in the government.

FOREIGN MISSIONARIES

Malawi has had a number of Protestant missionary societies ministering to its people, the majority of them denominational. An estimated 220 missionaries representing 30 agencies work in Malawi. Some missions have struggled to relinquish responsibility as the national churches have matured, and some Malawian churches still depend on overseas policy and funds. Mission agencies operating in Malawi include:

- Africa Evangelical Fellowship
- Assemblies of God
- Canadian Assemblies of God
- Church of Christ
- Church of the Nazarene
- Dutch Reformed Church
- Free Church of Scotland
- Global Field Evangelism
- Southern Baptist Convention
- United Society for the
  Propagation of the Gospel
- Universities' Mission to Central Africa
- World Outreach

These missions have handed the work to national churches. Expatriate workers, the majority of whom are involved in institutional work, generally work under the guidance of national churches. A number of smaller missions also work in Malawi.

National leaders feel there is a need to evaluate the continued presence of missionaries and missions in the country and to prepare the churches for a complete withdrawal of expatriate personnel and resources. To facilitate this transition, mission agencies need to emphasize post-graduate and leadership training in ministry, management, financial control, medicine, and education.

Continued legal registration of missionary societies as distinct from national churches creates a degree of tension. A number of parachurch organizations operate in Malawi, including:

- Africa Enterprise
- Bibles for Africa
- DAWN Ministries
- Every Home Crusade
- Hospital Christian Fellowship
- Institute for Church Growth
- Life Ministries
- Scripture Union
- World Vision

CHRISTIAN ACTIVITIES

Evangelism

A successful countrywide evangelistic campaign, *New Life for All*, was launched in 1968 by The Evangelical Association and 20 years later is still having an impact. Christians report that they have been blessed as they pray and witness together.

Several large evangelistic rallies have been held. Africa Enterprise held a mission in Blantyre in 1983 and in Lilongwe in 1987. Christ for All Nations held evangelistic rallies in Blantyre and Lilongwe and many decisions were made for Christ. Due to poor follow-up of converts, however, there has not been much evidence of church growth that resulted.

A number of parachurch organizations have ongoing evangelistic ministries. These include Life Ministry, Scripture Union, and Hospital Christian Fellowship.

Many of Malawi's present church leaders met God through the ministry of Students Christian Organization (SCOU). This organization works with the Bible Society to reach young people in schools and colleges through Scripture distribution.

Leaders have also identified the need to re-evangelize nominal Christians, and to mobilize the laity to reach out to those around them.

Broadcasting

An estimated 1,060,000 radio receivers were used in Malawi in 1983. Malawi Broadcasting Service offers time for religious programs. A religious broadcasting organization, Dzimvere Service and Christian Broadcasting Service, offers training through workshops. Dzimvere also uses drama and film as tools for evangelism.

The Southern Baptist Church has a media center that prepares programs for broadcasting. Transworld Radio, transmitting from

Swaziland, has an office in Blantyre that prepares programs in Chichewa for broadcast in Malawi.

Christian literature

The production of Christian literature in Malawi dates back to the end of the nineteenth century. By 1907, all three synods of the Church of Central Africa Presbyterian (CCAP) had their own printing presses to produce booklets for churches and mission schools.

Today there are three large publishing houses:

CLAIM, established in 1968, is a joint publishing organization involving 14 denominations and Christian organizations. It has 37 bookshops and literature kiosks across the country, and more than 200 book agencies, some deep in rural areas. CLAIM trains Christian writers and distributes Christian literature.

Montford Press and *Likuni Press* are Catholic publishing houses. They publish liturgical and devotional material and have also become instrumental in the development of Malawian literature. Montford Press publishes a monthly magazine, *Moni*, and Likuni Press a fortnightly newspaper, *Odini*, which include religious and secular news and views.

A monthly magazine, *Kuunika*, is produced by the Presbyterian church. Other Christian publishers are the Assemblies of God, the Baptist Mission in Malawi, and Malamulo Publishing House. Christian organizations with bookshops include the Africa Evangelical Church, the Seventh Day Adventist church and Scripture Union.

Bible translation and distribution

Translation of the Scripture into the Chichewa language began in 1900. The New Testament was published in 1907 and the whole Bible in 1922. This translation was revised in the 1960s, but is still in old Chichewa, which cannot be readily understood by most people today. A new translation is in its final stages.

People who speak Tumbuka and Ngondi now have complete Bible translations. The New Testament and Psalms in Lomwe, published in Mozambique, is not easily understood by the Malawian Lomwe. A translation based in Malawi is needed.

A New Testament was published in Chiyao by the Anglican church many years ago but is now out of print. A new translation is underway, and the New Testament is almost complete. The Gospel of John is available. Chisena is another language in which a translation is needed.

In 1987, the Bible Society distributed more than 61,556 Bibles, 52,478 New Testaments and more than 173,000 portions and selections.

The Bible Society, in cooperation with Scripture Union, has a program for youth. The have secured permission to visit every school in the country. Special selections of Scripture, particularly geared to meet the needs of youth, have been prepared for distribution, addressing subjects such as friendship and relationships, drugs, and fear of exams. Bibles for Africa, in cooperation with the Bible Society, is involved in this program of distributing 50,000 Bibles to schools. They are also distributing 95,000 New Testaments and 130,000 gospels in four major languages.

Social work

The government willingly accepts the churches as partners in development. Many denominations and churches are involved in social action. These include the Roman Catholic Church, the Anglican church, CCAP, the Seventh Day Adventist church, the Southern Baptist Church and the Africa Evangelical Church.

The Church of the Nazarene runs a vocational training school at Limbe. Faith Christian Services assists churches. The Christian Service Committee, the social arm of the Christian Council, raises funds abroad for community development and training programs. World Vision International runs more than 100 projects throughout Malawi, the majority of which are community-based development projects.

The estimated 800,000 Mozambican refugees present a challenge to the churches and relief organizations, and a number of Christian agencies serve them.

The Private Hospital Association of Malawi coordinates the 20 Christian hospitals in Malawi. Care is also provided at 130 health centers, dispensaries and health posts.

The church has been involved in secular education since the early days of missionary activity, when education was used as an instrument to build the church. It was also seen as a gateway to employment. Young people who had received training in mission schools soon found employment in the colonial government or with European planters or traders. Although literacy brought social status, there was unhealthy preference given to literates in the churches. It became normal practice in the Scottish missions to baptize only those who could read or write.

The Livingstonia synod of the CCAP was the leader in education in early days. In 1905, they were responsible for 834 schools, or 60 percent of all the schools in Malawi. Their Overtoun Institution became a renowned training center. By 1938, the Roman

Catholic Church had become the most influential in the educational field.

The primary school system was nationalized at independence, but the missions and churches retained control over secondary schools and training colleges. A deep commitment to train the country's youth remains in these institutions. The government participates by paying teachers' salaries.

Christian education

The history of training for the ministry dates back to the early years of the church. Overtoun Institution of the Livingstonia Mission, founded in 1903, and St. Michael's College of the Universities' Mission to Central Africa (Anglican) were two of the earliest colleges. Seminaries and colleges in Malawi include:

- African Bible College in Lilongwe
- Apostolic Faith Bible College in Blantyre
- Assemblies of God Bible Institute (Dedza)
- Baptist Bible Seminary in Lilongwe
- Free Methodist Bible School in Lilongwe
- Likubula Bible Institute in Blantyre
  (Africa Evangelical Church and United
  Evangelical Church, who also offer short
  term courses and seminars at a Bible
  Institute at Chididi)
- Lutheran Bible Institute at Lilongwe
- Namikango Bible School
  (Church of Christ)
- Nazarene Theological College
  (with a new campus in Lilongwe and a
  TEE ministry in Blantyre)
- Pentecostal Bible College (sponsored by
  the Pentecostal Church of Malawi and the
  Pentecostal Assemblies of Canada)
- St. Peter's Major Seminary, St. Anthony's
  Major Seminary and Kachebere Seminary
  (training for priesthood in the Roman
  Catholic Church)
- University of Malawi at Zomba
  (Department of Religious Studies)
- Voice of Prophecy Bible School
  (Seventh Day Adventist church)
- Zomba Theological College
  (trains ministerial students for the CCAP
  and the Anglican church)

Many of these Colleges and Bible Schools offer extension programs and correspondence courses. Theological Education by Extension in Malawi (TEEM) is an interdenominational ministry in Blantyre.

Parachurch organizations like World Vision, Life Ministry, United Church Lay Training Center and Evangelical Fellowship offer pastors' conferences, seminars, and training in evangelism and leadership.

Theological training has been westernized in approach. Most schools produce people trained in theology, but not necessarily in evangelism. Christian leaders hope to see contextualized training in evangelism, church growth, and identifying unreached peoples.

BIBLIOGRAPHY

Actea Directory of Theological Schools in Africa, 1985.

Africa South of the Sahara 1990, Europa Publications.

Cronje, J M., *Born to Witness*, NG Boekhandel.

Economist Intelligence Unit, *Country Report 1990/91*.

Economist Intelligence Unit: *Zimbabwe, Malawi, Quarterly Report No. 1, 1991*.

Fair, Denis, "Malawi: Building the Infrastructure," *Africa Insight*, No 1/87.

'M Passou, Dennis, *Directory of the Churches and Christian Organisations in Malawi*, Christian Communications Programme.

"Malawi, Focal Point of Islam's Revival in Southern Africa," *Muslim Views*, May 1987.

Malawi Demographic Survey 1982, National Statistical Office.

Malawi Statistical Yearbook 1985, National Statistical Office.

Mkolesia, Peter M., *A Survey of Interdenominational Co-operation in Malawi*.

Pauw, C.M., *Missions and Church in Malawi*, University of Stellenbosch.

Phiri, Isabel A., "The Future of Missions in Malawi," *International Review of Missions*, 1/87.

Reserve Bank of Malawi, *Annual Report*.

Third World Encyclopedia, Mansell.

Weller, John and Linden, Jane, *Mainstream Christianity to 1980 in Malawi, Zambia and Zimbabwe*, Mambo Press.

Zingani, Willie T., "Publishers of Christian Literature in Malawi", *Literature for Southern Africa*, Potchefstroom University for Christian Higher Education.

MAURITIUS

Co-edited by Mario Li Hing

Profile

Natural features: Mauritius is an Indian Ocean island lying south of the equator 800 km (500 miles) east of Madagascar. The island has 1,856 km^2 (720 square miles) of mountainous and volcanic land, and is surrounded almost entirely by a coral reef. Rodrigues, also a volcanic island, lies 585 km east of Mauritius, and has a land area of 104 km^2 (40 square miles). Two other dependencies, Agalega (two islands) and Cargados Carajos Shoals, formerly St. Brandon Islands (22 islets), have no permanent inhabitants.

Climate: Mauritius has a tropical maritime climate with two seasons. Cyclones occur between December and March. The climate along the coast is generally drier than the climate in the interior, which tends to be rainy and cool.

Population: 1,002,178 (1983 census); 1,100,000 (1990 estimate). Population density at 574 per km^2 is high (1988 estimate).

Ethnic groups: Four main groups: Franco-Mauritians, Creoles, Indians, and Chinese.

Languages: English is the official language, but Creole is the *lingua franca.*

Urbanization: 55%. Port Louis is the capital with a population of 150,000 (1988). Ten urban centers have sizable populations. Curepipe has a population of 64,000 (1983); Beau Bassin/Rosehill 93,000 (1983); Quatre Bornes 65,405.

Government: Mauritius is an independent sovereign state within the British Commonwealth, and is led by a coalition government that came into power in 1982. Elections are held every five years, with the most recent in 1987. The Prime Minister is Rt. Hon. Sir Aneerood Jugnauth.

Economy: Currency: 100 cents = 1 Mauritian rupee. Exchange rate: 15 Mauritian rupees per US$1 (1989 average). G.D.P. (1990) MR 34.9 billion. G.D.P per capita: MR 31,727 or US$2,115 (1990). Growth rate: 2.1%; average 1960-82, 9% in 1986; 5% est. for

1990. Inflation rate: 16% in 1990. Imports: US$1,589 in 1990. Exports: US$1,154 in 1990. Employment in agriculture: 28%. Agriculture as % of GDP: 13.2%.

Religion: (1983 census) Hindu 52.5%; Roman Catholic 25.8%; Muslim 16.6%; Protestant 1.5%; Anglican 0.5%; Uncommitted 3.1%.

HISTORICAL BACKGROUND

The earliest mention of Mauritius is in seventh-century Arab maritime charts, but the island remained uninhabited until the Dutch took occupation in 1598. After two attempts at settlement, they abandoned Mauritius in 1710.

The French arrived in 1715 and took formal possession. They administered the island until 1810, when the British captured it. The British freed slaves introduced by the French to work in the sugar plantations. Franco-Mauritian planters then recruited indentured labor from India. By 1861, two-thirds of the island's people were Indians.

From 1810 until independence in 1968, Mauritius was administered by the British Government. In 1947, a new constitution was introduced, based on the Westminster form of government. A general election was held (franchise dependent on literacy) and in 1948, a Legislative Assembly was formed. Although Britain maintained control of the island through the years, French influence remains strong and Franco-Mauritians still control most of the economy.

Between 1945 and 1959, the Indian community strengthened its political stakes on the island. Through legislation passed in 1958, Indians gained power that had been denied them, and the monopoly of the wealthy elite was weakened. Seewoosagur Ramgoolam, an Indian doctor, became the leader of the country.

Mauritius gained its independence from Britain in 1968 but remains a member of the British Commonwealth.

SOCIOECONOMIC CONDITIONS

The economy of Mauritius is a developing country success story. A socialist approach emphasized job creation and exports, resulting in rapid growth. The economy has been dependent on sugar for many years, but greater attention is being paid to manufacturing. This is slowly creating a more balanced economy.

Despite these moves to diversify the economy, sugar still occupies 90 percent of arable land, employs 28 percent of the labor force, and accounts for 40 percent of the country's export earnings. To some extent, this dependence on sugar has resulted in an economic position subject to climatic conditions and world sugar prices. Some 40 percent of the country's sugar crop is grown by owners who have formed themselves into cooperatives. The World Bank has called for further diversification.

Despite heavy reliance on one crop, Mauritius achieved a positive growth rate and inflation was kept low in the past. Recently, inflation has begun to rise.

Although tea and tobacco are grown and food crops are encouraged through cooperative efforts, Mauritius is still dependent on food imports. About 70 percent of the catch from the fishing industry is exported.

There is little real poverty among the people, but wealth in Mauritius remains concentrated among the elite. The pool of general employment opportunities is shrinking, while at the same time the number of unfilled skilled positions is growing.

Table 1: SOCIAL INDICATORS IN BRIEF

Total enrollment in education (1986)	208,947
% enrolled in primary schools	66%
% enrolled in secondary schools	33%
% enrolled in tertiary education	1%
Pupil/teacher ratio	34:1
Adult literacy rate	85%
No. of hospitals & health posts	33
Population per hospital bed	271
Population per nurse	2,900
Infant mortality rate per 1,000	32
Population in the 0 - 14 age group	33%
Population growth rate	1.42%
Life expectancy	68 years

Education

Mauritius has a high literacy rate because of the country's stress on education. Primary school is free but not compulsory, and approximately 95 percent of primary-school age children attend. Some 40 percent of school children continue on to secondary school.

Both state and private institutions provide education. Instruction is in English and French. Tertiary education is provided at teacher training colleges, technical and trade schools and at the University of Mauritius, where 1,000 students are registered. Many others study in foreign countries.

Health

Health services have rapidly improved. The government provides a health network through hospitals and clinics. Infant mortality rate is low (32 per 1,000), and population growth rate has decreased.

Mauritius lies in the Indian Ocean cyclone-belt and cyclones occasionally cause devastation. To minimize damage, reinforced houses are being built.

THE PEOPLE

There are no indigenous Mauritians—all are immigrants with origins in Europe, Africa or Asia. In the 1983 census, the population was classified into three broad groups of people: Indo-Mauritians, Sino-Mauritians, and the general population.

Indo-Mauritians

Indo-Mauritians are the largest ethnic group and comprise 68 percent of the population. The term "Indian" generally refers to people of Hindu faith (51%). Muslims account for approximately 17 percent of the population. Most Hindus descended from indentured labor, while the Muslims arrived as traders and formed a separate community.

Many languages are spoken by the Indian and Muslim populations. The larger language groups include:

- Bhojpuri (197,000)
- Hindi (111,134)
- Marathi (12,420)
- Tamil (35,134)
- Telegu (15,364)
- Urdu (23,572)

Sino-Mauritians

Most of the Chinese population are descendants of immigrant traders who arrived in the 19th and 20th centuries. Initially, they came from Canton, but the largest concentration of immigrants eventually came from Honan and were Hakka-speaking. According to the 1983 census, 21,000 Chinese live in Mauritius. Only 6,000 people use Hakka, Cantonese or Mandarin as their home language, with the remainder speaking Creole. Most of the Chinese live in and around Port Louis and work as retailers.

General population

This group includes all who are not of Indian or Chinese descent. Three percent of the population are Franco-Mauritians, the descendants of early French settlers. Much of the island's wealth is in their hands through their control of the sugar plantations and dominance in the professions.

English is rarely spoken in Mauritius, although it was a British possession before independence, is still a member of the British Commonwealth, and the official language is English. The *patois*, Creole, has become the language of the island.

Descendants of intermarriage in Mauritius are called Creoles. Mauritian society seems to follow a caste system based on skin color. Lighter-skinned Creoles, generally descendants of French traders, usually have had more opportunity for education and tend to work in commerce and the professions. Darker-skinned Creoles, generally descendants of early slaves, have had fewer opportunities and tend to be working class people.

RELIGIONS

Hinduism

Hindus practice two streams of philosophy in Mauritius. The Sanathan, who numbered 300,000 in the 1983 census, are orthodox in their belief in a trinitarian god, Brahma, and intermediate gods. The 100,000 Arya samajists profess monotheism.

Both philosophies are based on the three basic principles of Hinduism, namely *Karma* (the practice of good works), the notions of *Maya* (the illusion of the world), and *Samsara* (reincarnation). A caste system exists in the Hindu community.

Devout Hindus often have small shrines in the front gardens of their homes. Several villages have Hindu temples, with the largest and most ornate in Triolet.

Hindu religious leaders have become concerned about the inroads Christianity is making in the Hindu community and are seeking to be more relevant in their changing society.

Islam

About 17 percent of the population are Muslims, the vast majority of whom are Sunni Muslims (95%). Sunni Hanafites are the largest group, numbering over 150,000. There are 3,000 Meimons based at the Jummah Mosque in Port Louis, and about 5,000 Sunni Surtis. A small number belonging to a Muslim sect called Ahmadhya is active on the islands.

Buddhism

The number of Buddhists is declining. The 1983 census reported a total of 3,657 adherents.

Baha'i

The number of Baha'i listed in the 1983 census is 677, but the movement claims to have 6,000 followers.

Mormonism

Mormons, estimated to number 100 adherents, have gained official recognition as a church.

Jehovah's Witnesses

Jehovah's Witnesses are active on the island. A total of 2,525 witnesses belong to nine congregations.

NATIONAL CHURCHES

The government's policy of freedom of religion has nurtured the proliferation of divisions in all the major religions. This freedom respects the right of individuals to practice their own faith without proselytization by other groups. Christians use caution in their methods of evangelism.

Christianity on the island of Mauritius is predominantly Catholic, and the government regards the Catholic church as the representative of all the Christian denominations. Pentecostal and charismatic churches are growing rapidly while membership in the Catholic, Anglican and Presbyterian churches is declining.

Registration as a church is not easily gained. Five groups have achieved this status—Roman Catholics, Anglicans, Presbyterians, Seventh Day Adventists, and Mormons. Most other denominations are registered as "Friendly Associations." Registration as a church carries certain requirements like annual financial reporting, while benefits include the elimination of taxation.

Although there is no Christian council or association in Mauritius, there have been attempts to establish ecumenical relations. An informal annual meeting called "A Week of Unity" draws Roman Catholics, Anglicans, and Presbyterians together. Evangelicals hope to establish an Association of Evangelicals.

Table 2: RELIGIOUS AFFILIATION OF CHRISTIAN GROUPS

Roman Catholic Church	(1986 est) 297,557
Assemblies of God	(est) 25,000
Anglican church	(1983 census) 5,438
Seventh Day Adventist church	(1988 full members) 2,556
Other Pentecostal churches	(1983 census) 2,000
Christian Centers	(1989 est) 1,200
Presbyterian church	684
Evangelical church	(1989 est) 250
Full Gospel Church of God	(est) 150

Baptist church	(1989 est) 100

Roman Catholic Church

A Jesuit priest, Manoel d'Almeida, celebrated mass on the island in 1616, but Catholicism was not established until the Lazarite Fathers began work during French occupation. Catholicism became the island's official religion in 1721. It spread rapidly as slaves were baptized, and continued unabated even after the British gained possession of the territory. Early in the 19th century, the work was handed over to the Benedictines. They were later joined by Holy Ghost priests and Jesuits. In 1964, Mgr. Margeot became the first Mauritian bishop.

A charismatic influence is permeating the Catholic church, particularly among the Chinese community, bringing about more lay participation and greater spontaneity in worship. The church is establishing home cells throughout the island. Lay training programs are in operation.

Eighty-three priests work in Mauritius, of whom 48 are Mauritian. Sixty-three Mauritian priests and nuns work in 26 different countries. The church is responsible for 53 primary schools, 13 secondary schools, and a number of homes for the elderly.

The Catholic church in Mauritius is made up of a single diocese responsible directly to the Holy See. In 1986, there were an estimated 297,557 adherents, compared with 247,882 in the 1983 census. According to census figures, the church grew at an annual rate of 1.8 percent between the years of 1972 and 1983, while the population grew by 17 percent over the same ten-year period.

The visit of Pope John-Paul II in October 1989 improved relations between the government and the Catholic church.

Anglican church

The history of the Anglican church began with British occupation of the island in 1810. Services for the soldiers and sailors were held at the army barracks by the army chaplain, but attendees soon felt that a separate church was necessary.

Reverend H. Shepherd was appointed in 1812. He began to encourage his congregation to be involved in acts of mercy among blacks and Creoles. The church built schoolhouses which were also used for worship.

In 1850, the Mauritian Church Association was formed. This body became an important factor in the extension of missionary work in the colony and its dependencies.

The church grew rapidly under the leadership of Bishop V. Ryan, the first Bishop of Mauritius. When he arrived in 1854, there were two civil chaplains. By the time he left in 1867, there were 13 clergymen and 12 churches and chapels. Today, 17 congregations and preaching points (including Rodrigues) are served by 15 ministers.

Cyclone Carol struck the island in 1960 and damaged many school buildings. Six of the 17 churches were destroyed. The schools were reluctantly handed over to the government with the exception of one secondary school, St Andrews, with 1,000 pupils. The church also administers a home for the elderly.

The Anglican church has a declining membership. The 1962 census report recorded 6,705 adherents, and this number dropped to 5,438 by the 1983 census. This decline reflects the emigration of English-speakers after independence.

The diocese in Mauritius is one of five which form the Church of the Province of the Indian Ocean. The church set aside the year 1991 for special emphasis on evangelism.

Protestant churches

PRESBYTERIAN CHURCH OF MAURITIUS

The London Missionary Society was the first mission to work in Mauritius. In 1814 Rev. Jean Lebrun arrived. One of his first tasks was to establish a school. This work was later incorporated into the Church of Scotland.

The Presbyterian church unites the work of the Church of Scotland, the French Reformed Church and the Swiss Reformed Church. The first Presbyterian minister came to Mauritius in 1851. Not long after, St Andrew's Church was established. Today, six French-speaking churches are scattered across the island, and a church at Phoenix serves the English-speaking community. The 1983 census records a membership of 611 people. The Presbyterian church has gained government recognition as a church, and has five ministers, one of whom is involved in Theological Education by Extension (TEE) program.

SEVENTH DAY ADVENTISTS

Seventh Day Adventists came to minister in Mauritius in 1914. They currently have nine pastors and one evangelist caring for twenty churches. Although the official membership of the church is only 2,556 (census 3,070), including adherents increases this number to 10,000.

EVANGELICAL CHURCH OF MAURITIUS

This Evangelical Church of Mauritius started in 1969 when missionaries from the Africa Evangelical Fellowship arrived. They now have two churches, one at Rose Hill and one at Rose-Belle. About 200 church members and adherents attend. A small work has started at Flacq. A bookshop in Curepipe serves the Christian community of all denominations. Emmaus Bible Correspondence courses are conducted through the church.

BAPTIST CHURCH

The Foreign Mission Board of the Southern Baptist Convention has been in Mauritius since 1978. A small church has developed at Curepipe, and new outreaches at Grand Baie, Highlands and Quatre Bornes are developing. Two missionary couples assist in the ministry.

NON-DENOMINATIONAL CHURCHES

The Sino-Mauritian Evangelical Church (SMEC) is at Tombeau Bay with a membership of about 50. It has one church with a number of cell groups.

The Chinese Christian Fellowship has two churches with 200 members, and is pastored by a couple from Hong Kong.

Pentecostal churches

Assemblies of God was the first Pentecostal church established in Mauritius. It was introduced by Aime Cizeron in 1967. Several splits occurred in the early history of the denomination, resulting in a number of smaller Pentecostal groups.

The Assemblies of God Church has an estimated 25,000 members and adherents worshiping at 104 assemblies and preaching points across Mauritius and Rodrigues. Using bold outreach methods, this church continues to grow. Many attendees are converts from Hinduism, which is causing concern in the Hindu community. Assemblies at Rose Hill and Port Louis serve the Chinese community.

The church has used contextualization to reach Muslims. The Jummah prayer fellowship was started to pray specifically for the conversion of Muslims. Monthly meetings are held for ex-Muslim believers, and a number of people gather to worship using Arabic Bibles and musical forms.

A School of Ministries trains laity and clergy in programs ranging from basic Christian orientation to a B.A. in Religious Education or Bible. Fifteen centers around the island provide part-time studies and 66 full-time students are enrolled at the college at Rose Hill.

The Apostolic Faith Mission grew out of the study courses provided by the Pan African Bible College. They have one church in Port Louis.

Other Pentecostal churches include:

- Christian Charismatic Church
- Emmanuel Fellowship

- Full Gospel Church of God
  (includes *La Voix de la Deliverence*)
- Life Center Ministry

Christian Centers started as a breakaway from the charismatic movement in the Catholic church. About 95 percent of the converts join as a result of healing and deliverance. Five churches have a total of 1200 members. The work has also extended to Réunion and Madagascar. A training college operates at Curepipe.

FOREIGN MISSIONARIES

Few missionary societies send missionaries to Mauritius. It is difficult for expatriate workers to enter. Each registered church may apply for a one-year visa for one missionary family. There is no difficulty, however, in obtaining a three-month visa, and churches are using this method to obtain short-term lecturers for their Bible schools.

Missionary societies or churches that send missionaries or representatives to Mauritius include:

- Africa Evangelical Fellowship
- Southern Baptist Convention
- Presbyterian Church of Canada
- WEC International

Three Mauritians have been sent out by WEC International to work in other countries.

CHRISTIAN ACTIVITIES

Evangelism

Christians are free to witness in this multi-religious society and even house-to-house visits are permitted.

Opportunity for ministry in schools and on campuses is limited, although Christian students may meet together. Youth for Christ and Scripture Union are working with young people in Mauritius.

The *Jesus Film* is available in French and is shown across the island.

Christian education

Roman Catholics do not train for the priesthood in Mauritius. Those seeking to enter the Catholic church are sent to France for training. A pre-seminary formation course is offered in Mauritius.

Assemblies of God churches place great emphasis on training, and are preparing for a major evangelistic outreach to other islands. A central School of Ministry offers five programs ranging from correspondence courses in evangelism through to degree-level courses.

The Anglican church has a training center, St Paul's College, which has been in existence for many years. It was used to train clergy and laity but today it is dormant. It will be reopened as a provincial theological college.

The Seventh Day Adventist church had a college at Phoenix that trained pastors for Mauritius and other Indian Ocean Islands, but currently this college is not operating.

A Theological Education by Extension (TEE) program, Formation Biblique Theologique in Mauritius, currently trains 200 students. It is supported by the Anglican, Presbyterian and Catholic churches.

Other groups using TEE training methods and correspondence courses include the Baptist church and Apostolic Faith Mission. Youth for Christ and the Evangelical church offer Emmaus Bible Correspondence Courses.

Radio

In 1985, the people of Mauritius owned 250,000 radios. The country has a government-owned radio and television service. The government allows limited Christian exposure on the radio. The Seventh Day Adventist church offers a 10-minute program on Sunday evenings, and the Baptist church has a 20-minute weekly program. The Roman Catholic Church is also allotted time.

FEBA programs are transmitted from Seychelles. An inter-church committee has been formed to produce Creole and French programs.

Literature

The Mauritian government places great emphasis on education, and the new generation of Mauritians reads and converses in English and French. Christians have the opportunity to reach these young people with the gospel through the written word, but Christian literature is limited.

The need for literature in Creole has been under discussion for a number of years. Although there are literacy training courses teaching Creole, there is no orthography, and only the older generation would be served by Creole translations. The Bible Society is translating the New Testament into Creole, and the Gospel of Mark has been published as a test case.

Scripture Union distributes daily readings. Local secretaries within the denominations act as distributors. Scripture Union also serves as a wholesaler for its own publications.

Christian bookshops operating in Mauritius include:

- Bible Society (selling Bibles and Sunday School materials)
- Evangelical Church in Curepipe
- Christian Center in Curepipe
- Center Documentation in Rose Hill (Catholic)
- Center Catechetique in Rose Hill (Catholic)
- Center Pere Laval in St Croix
- Lamb of God (an interdenominational bookshop just opened in Port Louis)

The Catholic church publishes *la Vie Catholique*, a weekly newspaper. The Seventh Day Adventist church issues *Lien*, a quarterly newspaper. The Assemblies of God church's quarterly magazine is entitled *Missions*. The Anglican *Herald* is published twice yearly. Scripture Union distributes daily reading notes and sells other books at wholesale and retail prices. *Seve et Vigne* is published monthly by the Presbyterian church. Youth for Christ has begun a youth magazine called *Exit*.

RODRIGUES

The island of Rodrigues is a dependency of Mauritius. It is 500 km to the east and is 108 km^2 in area. Rodrigues has two representatives in the legislative assembly, one of whom is the minister for the island.

The population was 33,082 in the 1983 census and consists mainly of Creoles. The people are predominantly Catholic (97%) but the 1983 census reports church adherence as follows:

Roman Catholic	32,089
Anglican	193
Seventh Day Adventist	102
Assemblies of God	150
Other Pentecostal	64

Four priests in the Roman Catholic Church serve three parishes. Four primary schools are under the church's care, and responsibility for a secondary school is shared with the Anglican church.

A challenge facing the church in Rodrigues is the tendency to blend faith with traditional beliefs.

There are 178 Hindus and 140 Muslims in Rodrigues.

NEEDS IN MAURITIUS

Linked to a flourishing economy is a changing value system and a rising rate of divorce. AIDS (Aquired Immune Deficiency Syndrome) is spreading.

Drug addiction is becoming a problem in Mauritius. With ships calling at Port Louis from all parts of the world, drugs are easily accessible. Young people, especially, are tempted. While many Mauritians are able to read French and English, Christian material in any language is limited. Students on the university campus, colleges and schools need to hear the good news of Jesus Christ.

BIBLIOGRAPHY

Boodhoo, Sarita, *What's wrong with the Hindus?* Deen Bandhu Publications, 1981.

Dinan, Monique, *The Mauritian Kaleidoscope.*

Dioce'se de Port-Louis, *Annuaire du Dioce'se de Port-Louis*, 1989.

Economist Intelligence Unit, *Country Profile Mauritius 1990/91.*

EIU Country Report, No. 1, 1991.

Ellis, Roystan, *Guide to Mauritius*, Media House Publications.

Emmanuel, The Ven. G, Diocese of Mauritius.

Europa Publications, *Africa South of the Sahara 1989.*

Fleming, Rev. Francis, *Mauritius*, SPCK 1862.

Selvon, Sydney, et al, *Mauritius: Its People, Its Cultures*, Editions Arc-en-ciel.

PEOPLE'S REPUBLIC OF MOZAMBIQUE

Co-edited by Steven Hardy

Profile

Natural features: 779,380 km^2 (308,641 sq miles) of land on the east coast of Africa. The coastline extends for 2,470 kilometers (1,535 miles) from Tanzania in the north to South Africa in the south. Mozambique shares borders with six countries. The land is mostly low-lying plateau, and 45% of the area has an altitude of less than 1,000 meters (3,280 feet).

Climate: Except for the far south, Mozambique has a tropical climate. Temperature on the coast ranges from 23-27°C (73-81°F). Altitude moderates the temperature. Rain falls mainly between December and April, and is heaviest in the uplands, ranging up to 1,500 mm (59 inches) per year.

Population: 15.7 million (1990). Annual growth rate: 2.7%. Population density: 19 per km^2. About 46% of the population is in the 0-14 age group.

Ethnic groups: Nine major ethnic groups with many sub-groups.

Language and literacy: Portuguese is the official language. No common ethnic language. Literacy rate: 21%.

Urbanization: 10%. Capital: Maputo (1 million). Other cities: Beira (500,000), Tete, Nampula, Quelimane, Nacala.

Government: A socialist one-party state. Executive: President (Joaquim Chissano), party-central and executive committees. Legislative: People's assembly. Administrative subdivisions: ten provinces.

Economy: Currency: 100 centavos = one metical (MT; plural meticais), 860 MT = US$1 (Average for 1989). MT1101 in February 1991. GDP (1990): MT1012 billion (US$614.9 million). GNP per capita (1988 est): MT29,699. Growth rate in decline since 1982 but 3% in 1990. Defense spending accounts for 35% of annual budget. Trade (1989): imports $940 million, exports $110 million. Inflation (1990): 20%. Agriculture contributes 41% of GDP and employs 84% of labor force.

Religion: (est) Traditional 33%, Roman Catholic 22%, Protestant 14%, Muslim 13%, African Independent 5%, No stated religion and Atheists 10%, Other (Hindu, Baha'i etc.) 3%.

HISTORICAL BACKGROUND

The central factor throughout Mozambique's history has been its role as gateway to the interior.

The original inhabitants of Mozambique were the Khoisan people (Bushmen and Hottentots), who fled or were subdued as Bantu people began migrating from the north. These migrations of people began as early as 400 AD, and settlements of people were still taking place in the nineteenth century.

Arabs, who supposedly settled on the islands off the coast of Tanzania as early as the eighth century, made contact with African chiefs.

A lively trade in ivory, gold, and slaves was already in existence by the time the first Portuguese traders arrived in the late sixteenth century. The Portuguese concentrated on protecting and reinforcing trading settlements and Indian Ocean trade routes.

In 1890, the boundaries of Mozambique were established. In 1951, Mozambique became an overseas province of Portugal.

Nationalistic stirrings began after World War II. Frelimo (the Mozambique Liberation Front) was formed in 1962 as an amalgamation of small, exiled political groups. The movement began in the north, rapidly advanced, and gained control over much of northern and central Mozambique.

Mozambique finally secured independence after a military coup overthrew the dictatorship of Salazar in Portugal in 1974. On June 25, 1975, Samora Machel became the first president of the Marxist one-party People's Republic of Mozambique.

As the Portuguese colonial government had done virtually nothing to prepare Mozambique for independence, the situation in the years following 1975 became increasingly chaotic. Socialization in the ten administrative provinces began with Frelimo exercising its political dominance through local Party committees. These committees also served as disseminators of the central government's Marxist ideology.

The new regime nationalized land, schools, hospitals, commerce and industry, accelerating the mass emigration of Portuguese who had operated the economy and administration. Schools and social services were open to many Mozambicans for the first time.

Unfortunately, the Mozambican government lacked expertise to maintain the structures and industries it had nationalized. As new economic approaches failed to produce adequately, life became increasingly difficult for the people. Mozambique was further crippled by a series of natural disasters, including floods in 1977 and 1984 and a three-year drought beginning in 1984.

One of the facts of life in Mozambique is the on-going presence of war. For a few years after independence, Mozambique served as a political and military base for Zimbabwe's war of independence. The expenses of this war further exhausted the limited resources of Mozambique.

Perhaps the most tragic result of involvement in this struggle for another country's independence was the creation and maintenance by the Rhodesian Defense Force of a resistance movement within Mozambique called RENAMO (National Resistance Movement or MNR). Initially, this group served the interests of Rhodesia (as Zimbabwe was previously called) in destabilizing Mozambique. As an anti-government movement, it attracted followers among the Portuguese ex-colonists as well as those discontented with the political and economic policies of the Marxist-socialist government of Mozambique.

After Zimbabwe obtained its independence in 1980, several years of relative calm came to Mozambique. Unfortunately, rebel activities and armed attacks have increased in recent years. The initial goal of RENAMO seemed to be to modify and not to overthrow the government. Since 1984, however, they have no apparent defined political policy nor the ability or even desire to run a country if they did gain power. Their goal seems to be to make Mozambique ungovernable.

Although the rebels claim to control large sections of the country, it is more accurate to say they have made most of the country into a "no-man's land." Periodic attacks on economic and communications structures have made road and rail transportation impossible in most areas of the country.

There is little sympathy for the RENAMO movement within the country, and Mozambican Christians speak of "escaping" from the areas rebels claim to hold. According to a report done for the U.S. State Department in April, 1988, RENAMO forces have systematically destroyed villages, stolen crops and abducted people to serve as laborers, burden-bearers or sexual partners. Relief agencies report that RENAMO has regularly destroyed relief goods rather than let them be delivered to those who are suffering. Because of this pattern of systematic atrocities, there is no visible international support for this movement.

According to reports, in RENAMO-controlled areas, a tribal system of government is reintroduced and crops planted. But towns are abandoned, highways are overgrown, medical care is nonexistent, and education grinds to a halt. According to a UNICEF report, 3,500,000 people are affected and in need of food aid. Two-thirds of the population live in absolute poverty.

Because of the guerrilla aspects of war and the atrocities that occur on all sides, an estimated 1.5 million refugees have fled into neighboring countries. About 750,000 refugees have fled Mozambique and temporarily settled in Malawi, 500,000 in South Africa, 100,000 in Zimbabwe, 40,000 in Zambia, and 25,000 in Swaziland. Another three million people have been displaced within Mozambique. Many of these refugees are Christians.

Disaster of this dimension requires a coordinated effort from the many aid organizations working in the country, but the difficulties involved in distributing food aid are daunting. Involving 50 countries and millions of dollars, a relief effort has eased but not halted Mozambique's emergency situation. Aid programs and economic reforms have improved the supply of food to the cities but famine in rural areas may go undetected for months because of inaccessibility due to the war. Relief workers feel that peace is the only real antidote.

Efforts are being made to promote dialogue with RENAMO, but major difficulties remain. Although the war continues, it is questionable whether RENAMO could be defeated on the battlefield because of the guerrilla nature of its tactics.

Several positive steps have been taken by the Mozambican government, however, that may undercut internal discontent. One such step has been to open up markets and decentralize farming, industry and housing by limiting state control. The government has asked churches and others for help in reconstructing schools, hospitals and relief centers. It has accepted the presence of many relief agencies to help alleviate the suffering.

The introduction of a new constitution has been widely praised and promises the introduction of a new and more liberal era. The constitution allows for political pluralism and Frelimo will need to decide whether they are prepared to fight an election. Although a partial ceasefire has been agreed, Frelimo does not appear to be honoring the agreement and terrorist acts continue.

THE PEOPLE

The peoples of Mozambique are not part of a unified social structure. Mozambique's nine main ethnic groups are summarized in Table 1.

**Table 1: ETHNIC GROUPS IN MOZAMBIQUE
AS A PERCENT OF THE TOTAL POPULATION**

Makhuwa-Lomwe (Makhuwa, Lomwe, Chuwabo, Marendje)	45.2%
Tsonga (Changana, Ronga, Tshwa)	22.3%
Nsenga-Sena (Nsenga, Nyungwe, Sena, Kunda, Nyanja)	15.3%
Shona (Shona-Manika, Ndau, Teve)	6.6%
Chopi	2.9%
Makonde	2.0%
Gitonga	1.9%
Yao	1.7%
Swahili (Swahili, Kimwani, Koti)	0.9%
Other (Portuguese, Swazi, Zulu)	1.2%

In the north, the Makhuwa-Lomwe peoples are in the majority. They are mainly matrilineal and are agriculturalists used to a more mobile type of crop production.

The people in the southern and central areas of Mozambique are largely patrilineal. Along the Zambezi River, the Nsenga-Sena are the predominant group, and in the central areas, the Shona are in the majority. In the south, the main group is the Tsonga, who have traditionally practiced a more settled type of crop and pastoral agriculture. Many of the smaller groups are related to larger groups in adjacent countries.

SOCIOECONOMIC CONDITIONS

At independence, Mozambique inherited a weak economy that was based on the export of raw materials and served Portuguese interests.

In 1975, the new government brought many changes, including the nationalization of industry and the socialization of the agricultural sector. A mass exodus of the Portuguese and their skills took place, and Mozambique lost foreign investment. A rapid decline in the country's growth rate followed.

In 1984, the government made changes to include limited private enterprise. In 1987, the government made an agreement with the IMF and the World Bank to devalue the currency, lift food subsidies, and introduce a greater degree of free enterprise. The government is now committed to economic reform and long-term recovery shows signs of hope. Privatisation is continuing to the extent that less than half of industrial output is generated by state enterprises. Foreign aid remains the lifeline of the economy.

Agriculture

Agriculture is the main economic activity in Mozambique, accounting for 84 percent of employment, 70 percent of foreign exchange earnings, and 41 percent of the gross domestic product (1987). Drought, the displacement of people, destruction of crops by guerrilla forces and the theft of crops by warring factions has resulted in total devastation of the countryside in many areas of Mozambique.

Education

At independence, 93 percent of the people were illiterate. Education for people in rural areas was almost non-existent. The Frelimo government strongly emphasized schooling, and by 1984, the literacy rate had risen until about 20 percent of the overall population, 11 percent of rural men, and 3.8 percent of rural women were literate.

Economic decline and conflict, however, forced many schools to close. By 1986, the total number of schools had been reduced by 36 percent. The education of about half a million children has been disrupted.

In the schools that remain, only Portuguese is used, but this is being reconsidered in light of the official recognition in 1988 of the multiplicity of languages spoken in Mozambique.

Health services

Prior to independence, little health care was available to rural people. When the government nationalized health care at independence, the number of doctors in the country dropped from 500 to 80. The emphasis was changed from curative to preventive health care. Health posts were established and health care workers were trained.

Despite gains made, the government estimates that 40 percent of children never reach their fifth birthday. Infant mortality ranges from 100-200 per 1,000 live births. Diarrheal diseases and malnutrition are the main killers.

Overall health in Mozambique has deteriorated. About 30 percent of Mozambique's health facilities operating in 1981-82 no longer function as a result of the war. Some 700 health units, serving two to three million rural people, have been affected.

UNREACHED PEOPLES

In 1968 the *World Christian Handbook* estimated the total Protestant population of Mozambique to be less than 2 percent. All but one of the mission stations in the country at that time were in the southern part of the country. Thus 75 percent of the country, with 80 percent of the population, was without a Protestant witness.

Since independence, large scale destabilization of the country-side has taken place. People have been moved into collective villages, and others have fled the horrors and difficulties resulting from the war. This social upheaval has resulted in widespread turning to God among tribes who have traditionally been regarded as unreached. Refugees in neighboring countries are encountering Christianity for the first time. Christian refugees serve as impromptu missionaries scattered inside and outside the country, sharing the gospel wherever they go.

The largest group of unreached people are the Makhuwa-Lomwe tribes in the north of Mozambique, making up 45 percent of the population. An estimated 20 percent of them are Muslims. Due to evangelistic outreach by the United Baptists, the Church of Christ and the Assemblies of God churches, large numbers of the Makhuwa-Lomwe people are becoming Christians despite the difficulties of the war.

About one million Muslims in the north and northeast of the country number have limited exposure to Christianity. They include Swahili, Koti, Makonde, Kimwani and Yao ethnic groups. German Brethren workers in Tanzania make contact accross the border, and a few are becoming Christians. Some of these attend Bible school in Tanzania.

The Ndau, living in the west adjoining Zimbabwe, are also relatively unreached.

STATUS OF CHRISTIANITY

Colonization of Mozambique began in the sixteenth century, and Catholic priests arrived with the Portuguese traders. Dominican missionaries were the first to come in 1506, followed by Jesuits. Until the late nineteenth century, their activities were confined to the southern part of the country.

The first Protestants came in 1820 when a British Methodist missionary arrived, but this work was soon abandoned. A number of missionaries arrived in the late 19th century. The United Methodist Church established work at Inhambane in 1879, followed by the American Board Mission in 1883.

The Presbyterian church, working over the border in South Africa, extended its work to Mozambique in 1887. Another early entrant was the Anglican church, which started work among the Yao in 1893.

Protestant ministry under the Catholic-dominated Portuguese government was extremely difficult and restricted. In other countries, a more tolerant attitude towards Protestant missions and

Protestant churches emerged following the Second Vatican Council. Within Mozambique, however, the years between 1960 and 1975 were the most difficult for Protestant churches.

It is generally felt that Protestant churches have been given much more liberty since independence than under the earlier Catholic regime. Religion in a Marxist-Leninist state is not easy, however, and for the first few years after independence (1975 - 1979), life was difficult. Schools and hospitals operated by churches and missions were nationalized, and churches that met in these facilities were closed. This was done to separate social services from the church. Some clergy and church members were imprisoned and mistreated. Laws forbade holding church services anywhere except in authorized buildings, and Sunday schools, women's work and youth work were prohibited.

Many churches, however, managed to continue as before. Since singing had always been a major part of youth meetings, young people simply began to call themselves "mixed choirs" rather than Christian youth groups. Government control of churches never reached the point of censoring sermons or appointing "approved" pastors for churches.

In December 1982, President Samora Machel summoned leaders of all faiths to ask for help in the rehabilitation of the country. Since then, the government has shown a more conciliatory attitude towards Christians.

In June 1984, the Director of Religious Affairs informed church leaders that recognized denominations would be granted permission to rebuild churches and that training centers could be developed. Further concessions were granted in June 1988 when the government announced that churches or places of worship that had been taken over in 1975 would be handed back.

The present situation

Today, a much greater freedom of religion exists in Mozambique. There is now no sign of government persecution or restriction on the church and on personal witnessing. Atheistic propaganda is quietly being discontinued. Churches are growing rapidly and are full of young people. Christians are building churches all over the country, including in communal villages, although the formation of new church groups is still discouraged.

Hospitals and schools for Mozambicans were started by missions and churches, but were nationalized at independence. All churches that met on the premises were closed, but some are gradually being opened again today. Though government spokesmen have stated that social institutions will not be handed back to the churches, the government's request for the United Methodist

Church to take joint responsibility for a previously nationalized hospital may be a sign that these policies are being reconsidered.

Relationships between the government and the churches are conducted through the Director of Religious Affairs. Umbrella bodies carry weight in representing general subjects of interest shared by all the churches. Protestant churches are loosely grouped together under two basic umbrella bodies, although many churches do not belong to either of these groups:

- The Christian Council of Mozambique
  (not affiliated with the World
  Council of Churches)
- The Association of Independent Christian
  Churches in Mozambique.

The government does not require that a church group belong to a recognized umbrella body. It is, however, necessary that each church be a "registered" church. To obtain recognition, denominations present their constitution and leadership to the Department of Religious Affairs. No restrictions have been placed on receiving foreign monies, materials or workers.

Although not singled out for persecution, Christians in the many areas where civil war continues are not excluded from hardship and suffering. Since the beginning of 1987, RENAMO guerrillas are reported to have killed three religious workers and abducted 19 priests and missionaries. Pastors and church workers have been killed or have starved to death. As villages have been burned, many churches have been burned with them.

Many who left the church at independence to follow Marxist philosophy are returning. Christians have a visible hunger for the Bible and systematic teaching, creating a need for Bible schools and lay training. The low literacy rate presents a difficulty to the church. Education has been firmly in the hands of the government, but it is now possible to hold literacy classes within the framework of the church, perhaps combining such classes with practical skills training for believers.

NATIONAL CHURCHES

Due to unsettled conditions and poor communication, statistics for churches in Mozambique are almost impossible to obtain. But statistics are not needed to see that social unrest has created a hunger for God. Thousands are seeking to know God. All churches report tremendous growth. In the future, God will reveal what he has been doing in his church during these years of trial and refining. In the meantime, many church denominations can only broadly estimate the number of congregations and members.

Estimated religious affiliation is listed in Table 2 and denominational membership in Table 3.

Table 2: ESTIMATED RELIGIOUS AFFILIATION

Traditional	33
Catholic [2]	22
Protestant [1]	14
Muslim	13
African Independent churches [1]	5
No stated religion	
Other (Hindu Ba'hai, etc.)	3

[1] *Includes children of church-going families*
[2] *Includes baptized children*

Table 3: MEMBERSHIP OF LARGE DENOMINATIONS

Roman Catholic Church	3,300,000
United Baptist Church	160,000
Evangelical Assemblies of God	120,000
Presbyterian Church of Mozambique	100,000
Anglican church	62,000
United Methodist Church	60,000
African Assemblies of God	50,000
Church of Christ in Zambezia North	25,000
Free Methodist Church	20,000
International Assemblies of God	20,000
Nova Alianca (Brethren)	20,000
Seventh Day Adventist church	20,000
Church of God World Missions (Full Gospel)	18,000
Church of the Nazarene	8,000
Pentecostal Holiness Church	8,000
CCAP	7,000
Congregational Church	7,000
Reformed church	6,200
Apostolic Faith Mission	6,000
Methodist Church of Southern Africa	6,000
Church of Christ in Beira	5,000
Convention Baptist Church	5,000

Roman Catholic Church

Dominican priests arrived as early as 1506 but it was not until the arrival of Jesuits in 1560 that missionary activity began, concentrating mainly in the southern areas. In the late nineteenth century, Catholic missionaries began work north of the Save River.

By the year 1900, only 0.6 percent of the population (including the Portuguese) were professing Catholics. By 1970, 17 percent of the population were Catholics. At that time, 50 out of 780 religious and secular priests were African. Of a total of 1,224 sisters, 165 were African.

The Catholic church was severely affected when the country gained independence, largely because they were seen by many as an arm of the colonial regime. They had done little to Africanize the church, and when the Portuguese were overthrown, there were no African bishops. During the first year of the revolution, 150 religious brothers, 300 priests and 950 nuns left the country and the church was divested of its schools and medical work. Many Catholics became confused and abandoned the faith. The church reported an 80 percent drop in church attendance.

The church is gradually becoming more "Africanized." In 1974, the first African archbishop was appointed. But even today, only 30 of 230 priests are Mozambicans. The membership of the Catholic church is about 3.3 million. In addition to the priests, there are 64 brothers and 380 nuns.

The Catholic seminary in Maputo has 18 men in training. A number of applicants have been turned away because of a lack of accommodation. Permission has been granted to build an institute of higher learning in Matola outside of Maputo.

Anglican church (Igreja Anglicana)

Anglican witness began a century ago when Reverend William Johnson and Charles Janson arrived on the eastern shores of Lake Niassa to work among the Yao. The first permanent mission was established at Unango in 1893. By 1900, the church had grown to 200 members.

Work in the south was established through the eastward movement of Anglicans from South Africa into the districts of Maputo, Gaza and Inhambane. In 1893, the Anglican church consecrated Reverend W. E. Smythe as the first bishop of the diocese of Southern Mozambique. By 1970, 45,000 members or 5 percent of the population attended.

At independence, 28 of 117 churches were closed, but there is still testimony of vibrant life in the church. After the Cathedral at Maciene had been closed for more than five years, permission to reopen it was granted and celebrated as a joyous occasion. A report from this district notes that all church buildings are too small for the congregations that use them.

By 1980, there were 62,000 members in the Anglican church. About 60 percent of the people participating in the life of the church are young people.

Protestant churches

UNITED BAPTIST CHURCH
(IGREJA UNIAO BAPTISTA)

The United Baptist Church (*Igreja Uniao Baptista*) is the result of a merger of Evangelical churches in the north and Scandinavian Baptist churches in the south.

In the late 1930s, the South African General Mission, which is now the Africa Evangelical Fellowship, took over the work of the Church of Scotland that had begun in the north in 1912. The work in the south was started by Mozambicans returning from the mines in South Africa, and in 1928, the Scandinavian Free Baptists accepted responsibility for the work.

Missionaries in the north were obliged to leave when the Portuguese closed the mission in 1959, but the church continued to grow during both the colonial regime and the post-independence era. From 1960 to 1982, the number of churches in the north increased from 45 to 450, while members increased from 3,000 to 44,000.

This church group is now the largest Protestant denomination in the country. Today, over 100,000 United Baptists worship in Nampula province alone. The work in the south has also grown rapidly, and includes some 150 congregations. Total membership is now about 160,000.

Reports indicate a visible hunger to learn about the Bible. Christians are asking for literature, training and Bible instruction. The church has recently started a Bible school and family training center in Maputo, and sees leadership training as its primary goal.

UNITED METHODIST CHURCH
(IGREJA METODISTA UNIDA)

The United Methodist Church was started in 1879. Its followers are mainly Tshwa in the Inhambane area. The 60,000 affiliated members worship in more than 900 congregations.

A recent agreement with the government calls for joint operation of a 200-bed hospital and its clinics, which were previously nationalized at independence. The church feels their agreement with the government could become a prototype for others.

PRESBYTERIAN CHURCH OF MOZAMBIQUE
(IGREJA PRESBITERIANA DE MOCAMBIQUE)

Presbyterian Church of Mozambique dates back to 1887, when the Swiss Mission decided to extend its work to include the Tsongas in Mozambique. In 1945, the church assumed its own financial responsibility, and in 1962, it became autonomous. From 1972 to 1974, the church suffered at the hands of the Portuguese.

One of its leaders was killed in a concentration camp. Today, the church has about 100,000 members.

CONGREGATIONAL CHURCH
(IGREJA CONGREGACIONAL UNIDA DE MOCAMBIQUE)

The Congregational Church had its origins in 1883 in the work of the American Board Mission. Work began in the Inhambane area. In 1919, the first Mozambican was ordained and placed in charge of the young church. Despite persecution, the church continues to experience and demonstrate the power of new life in Christ.

In 1967, the UCCSA (United Congregational Churches of Southern Africa) was formed, and the church became the responsibility of this body. Today, over 7,000 members and adherents are shepherded by 18 ministers and evangelists.

CHURCH OF THE NEW COVENANT IN CHRIST
(NOVA ALIANCA)

Church of the New Covenant in Christ (*Nova Alianca*) is a Brethren church headed by Domingos Meque, a Sena. From its inception in 1970, it has grown rapidly and now has about 20,000 members.

Pentecostal churches

The Evangelical Assemblies of God was started in 1911 by Paolo Xhosa. Xhosa was a young convert who had become a Christian through the Pentecostal Assemblies of Canada's work among miners in South Africa. Austin Chawner, a Canadian who trekked into Mozambique from South Africa as early as 1927, co-ordinated and organized this work among the miners. In 1934 he married Ingred Lokken, a Norwegian missionary, and their marriage led to a merger between Norwegian and Canadian Pentecostal work, forming the basis of the present Evangelical Assemblies of God of Mozambique.

Today, the Assemblies of God has about 120,000 members distributed among more than 600 assemblies. Reverend Lourenco Mulungo of Maputo pastors the largest Changana Church with some 19,000 members in 106 cell groups. Reverend Dino Amade leads the Central Portuguese language church in Maputo with some 6,000 members in 40 cell groups.

The church runs a two-year Bible school in Changana that is over a decade old, and in cooperation with the Pentecostal Assemblies of Canada, recently began a three-year Portuguese language Bible school program.

There are other large Assemblies of God groups, including the African Assemblies of God (*Assembleia de Deus Africana*) with an estimated 50,000 members; and the International Assemblies of God (*Assembleia de Deus Internacional*) with an estimated 20,000 adherents in some 400 congregations.

African independent churches

Because of government opposition, African independent denominations and churches have had difficulty establishing themselves. Nevertheless, about 100 officially recognized groups exist, some of them very small. A number of them broke off from existing churches, while others are imported from neighboring countries. One of the larger groups is the Church of the Twelve Apostles, with numerous churches throughout the country. Others include:

- African Apostolic Church
  (Johane Marambe)
- Igreja Luso-Africana
  (breakaway from Swiss Mission)
- United Church of Ethiopian South Africa

FOREIGN MISSIONARIES

Most expatriate missionaries left at independence, but since 1982, the country has slowly opened up once again to foreign workers. Due to a lack of security at the present time, placement of missionaries is limited to secure cities and towns.

A "contract" with a recognized church group makes it possible for an expatriate missionary to obtain a resident permit for two to six years, after which permits are reviewed. In principle, all missions planning to work in evangelism, church planting or leadership training in Mozambique should be invited by a registered church or official government organization. In practice, however, the Director of Religious Affairs now considers each request to work in Mozambique on its own merits.

Because Mozambique is in desperate need of international aid, Christian organizations and missions working in relief and development have negotiated their own contracts directly with the government. The government favors those organizations which emphasize local self-sufficiency. In many instances, supplies of food, clothing and equipment have opened the way for evangelistic ministry.

A number of foreign Christians have also come into Mozambique by accepting government contracts for different kinds of service within the country.

About 40 to 50 missions and parachurch agencies are based in Mozambique. Others are based outside Mozambique, bringing in supplies and evangelistic teams.

Those based in Mozambique include:

- Africa Evangelical Fellowship
- Africa Inland Mission
- ADRA (Adventist Relief)
- AirServ (secular cousin to Missionary Aviation Fellowship)
- American Board (Congregational Missions)
- Brazilian Baptist Convention
- Caritas
- Christian Missions in Many Lands (Emmaus courses)
- Feed My People International
- Jesus Alive Ministries
- Living Hope Mission
- Mennonite Central Committee
- Mission to Mozambique
- Norwegian Pentecostal Church
- Pentecostal Assemblies of Canada
- Reformed Church of RSA
- Southern Baptist Foreign Mission Board
- Swedish Free Baptists
- TEAM (The Evangelical Alliance Mission)
- United Methodist Missions
- Volksmission (German Assemblies of God)
- World Relief (U.S. National Association of Evangelicals)
- World Vision International
- Wycliffe Bible Translators
- Youth with a Mission

Parachurch groups based outside the country include:

- All Nations Gospel Publishers
- Bibles for Africa
- Evangelical Aid
- Far East Broadcasting Association
- Frontline Fellowship
- Global Literature Lifeline
- Jimmy Swaggart Ministries
- Open Doors
- Portuguese Radio Mission
- Scripture Gift Mission

- Scripture Union
- TEAR Fund
- Trans World Radio
- Inter-Varsity Press, Brazil
  (Alianca Biblica Universitaria)

CHRISTIAN ACTIVITIES

Evangelism

The pattern of evangelism in the past was intense activity in the south, partial penetration of the center of the country, and total neglect of the north. This imbalance resulted in the north being relatively untouched by the gospel. Today, the church is beginning to penetrate these areas previously untouched by Christianity.

The church in Mozambique has grown through deep adversity, first through the period of Portuguese colonialism, then through the Marxist revolution, and now through civil unrest. The national church multiplied despite trials, proving it can accomplish the task of evangelism without outside help. Outside organizations need to be cautious, and recognize the desire and ability in the national church to evangelize the people of Mozambique.

In addition to outreach through local churches, a number of organizations have been involved in evangelism in city-wide campaigns. Regulations that limit the holding of meetings to church buildings are not as strictly applied as they used to be, but this varies from area to area. Jesus Alive Ministries recently held large tent campaigns in Chimoio and Beira, and many decisions for Christ were recorded. Through previous campaigns, many new churches formed. Other evangelistic agencies include Christ for All Nations and Gospel Literature Lifeline. Most of the mass evangelistic campaigns have been held in the larger cities.

It is now possible to visit prisons and hospitals if this ministry is part of a recognized church.

Christians minister to refugees in surrounding countries. Refugee camps in South Africa have full-time workers who minister to peoples' physical needs as well as their spiritual needs.

Broadcasting

Radio as a means of evangelism appears to be an effective method of reaching the people, particularly the urbanized.

The government sees radio as an effective medium to communicate with the people and encourages its use. Short wave radios are manufactured in Maputo. In rural areas, it is difficult to get batteries for radios, but people rely on electricity in the cities. A government survey showed that in 1981, one out of two urban homes had a radio. In the rural areas, only one in eight families had a radio.

Before independence, the Roman Catholic Church was granted time on the national radio station, but this ceased at independence.

Trans World Radio, transmitting from its station in Swaziland, has three daily programs in Portuguese. It also transmits programs in Changana, Chitshwa and Lomwe. Nine participating church and mission groups prepare the programs.

Far East Broadcasting Association (FEBA), transmitting from its station in Seychelles, beams programs into Mozambique daily. The signals into Mozambique are strong and heard clearly throughout the country. One of the missions broadcasting daily over FEBA, the Portuguese Radio Mission, reports a good response from the estimated 200,000 listeners. Inquirers initially receive a Gospel of Mark and a correspondence study course.

It is also possible to pick up transmissions from neighboring countries such as South Africa and Swaziland, where religious broadcasts can be understood by English speakers, Changana or Nguni-based language users.

Bibles and Christian literature

Churches are appealing for theological training material, liturgical books, and song books. In view of the low adult literacy rate, simple reading material is also required. Many churches receive donations of food and clothing, but spiritual food needed for new Christians to grow—Christian literature—is seldom sent.

The National Institute for Books and Records controls the import and sale of books. Although there is no restriction on imports, a lack of foreign exchange makes it necessary for books to be donated. Furthermore, importing books must be organized through a recognized church.

Mozambique Bible Society (MBS) in Maputo regularly stocks Bibles. Although stocks are allocated to the northern areas, communication problems make delivery of the stocks very difficult. A 16 percent import duty and 3 percent sales tax must be paid on incoming stocks (even if donated).

The United Methodist Church runs two bookshops in Mozambique, one in Maputo, and the other in the Inhambane district. Both have limited stock. The Bible Society in Maputo sells hymnbooks and Scriptures in its bookshop, and the Presbyterian, Assemblies of God and New Alliance churches have book depots in Maputo. Book depots linked to local churches are a good way to distribute literature.

Sasavona Publishers (Evangelical Presbyterian Church) publishes in Tsonga (Changana) and Tshwa (Chitshwa). Their publications include hymnals, booklets and books like a Bible dictionary in Chitshwa. They also act as distributors for publications of other churches and missions.

Bibles for Africa has printed 20,000 New Testaments in Lomwe, 20,000 New Testaments in Portuguese, and 20,000 study booklets. They are planning to supply 25,000 New Testaments to northern areas of Mozambique.

All Nations Gospel Publishers distributes free Gospel booklets in Lomwe, Sena, Tonga, Tsonga, Chitshwa and Yao languages. They report many mail responses.

Inter-Varsity Press of Brazil distributes free Bible commentaries and other literature to pastors, seminary students and seminary teachers using a TEAR Fund grant from Europe.

Biblecor produces Bible study material in Yao. WEC distributes a Portuguese news sheet called CEDO. CAVA (Christian Audiovisual Action) publishes material in Sena and Portuguese.

Other agencies in production and distribution include:

- Church of the Nazarene
- Emmanuel Mission Press
- Free Methodists
- Frontline Fellowship
- Global Literature Lifeline
- Open Doors
- Scripture Gift Mission

The many languages and dialects in Mozambique make it very difficult for all people to hear the Scriptures in their own tongue. Scriptures are available in the following languages:

- *Bitonga:* The New Testament (NT) was translated in 1897, and Old Testament (OT) portions in 1902. The full Bible is now available.
- *Chopi:* The Gospels were published in 1983.
- *Chuwabo:* The NT was translated in 1978 by the Roman Catholics.
- *Lomwe:* The NT was translated in 1930. MBS is currently working on a new translation.
- *Makhuwa:* The NT was translated in 1977, and the Bible in 1983 by the Roman Catholics.
- *Manika:* The NT was translated in 1908. People now use the Shona Bible.
- *Ndau:* The NT was translated into the Changa dialect in 1949, and the whole Bible in 1957; a revision is in progress.

- *Ngulu:* OT portions and the NT were translated by the Roman Catholics in 1897.
- *Nyungwe:* Portions of Scripture were translated by the Roman Catholics in 1897. The Bible Society is doing a translation.
- *Podzo:* Portions of Scripture were translated in 1897.
- *Portuguese:* The full Bible is available.
- *Ronga (Chironga):* The Bible was first translated in 1923. A revision of the NT is in progress.
- *Sena:* Portions of Scripture were translated in about 1897 by the Roman Catholics but were only available in duplicated form. In 1981 the Catholics printed a NT in Sena, but few evangelical churches make use of this translation. A new translation of Mark recently published by Emmaus Bible School was well received.
- *Shona:* The full Bible is available. A revision is in progress.
- *Tsonga (Changana):* The Bible was first translated in 1907 and revised in 1929. A new revision is in progress.
- *Tshwa (Chitshwa):* The Bible was published in 1910 and revised in 1955.
- *Yao:* The Bible was translated in 1920. The NT was revised in 1952.

Not all of these translations are readily available. The Mozambique Bible Society currently distributes Scripture in Tsonga (Changana), Shona, Chitshwa, Portuguese and Lomwe. The Yao NT is available. The Bible Society also reports sales of Russian, Hungarian and Chinese Bibles.

The Bible Society now works in the Ilomwe, Nyungwe, Chuwabo and Gitonga languages. Work in Chironga and Chopi languages is progressing. Wycliffe Bible Translators has begun translation in the Kimwani language.

In 1987, 12,443 Bibles, 11,965 New Testaments and 7,185 Scripture portions were distributed. This compares with 62,013 Bibles and 33,983 New Testaments distributed in 1986. This large drop in the number of Bibles and New Testaments sold and distributed is largely due to the devaluation of the local currency that affected the Bible Society as well as potential purchasers.

Distribution of the Scriptures presents problems. It can take up to six months for parcels dispatched to the northern and central provinces to reach their destination.

Christian education

The greatest need facing Mozambican churches today is the training of church leadership. Seminaries and Bible schools have many more applicants than openings.

Ricatla Seminary is operated by the Christian Council for Mozambique. Cooperating churches are the Presbyterian church, the United Methodist Church, the Congregational church, the Church of Christ and the Wesleyan church. Ricatla currently has 42 students enrolled.

The Roman Catholic Church has a seminary with 18 students in Maputo, the Anglican church has a seminary in Niassa, and the Seventh Day Adventist church has a seminary near Beira with about 40 students.

The Church of the Nazarene has a theological college in Gaza province, with 40 students. The Presbyterian church has a four-year evening course in theology for laity in Maputo.

The United Baptist Church has a residential seminary near Maputo with 11 students. They also maintain an evening Bible institute with 30 students in Maputo, have extension Bible classes in Quelimane, Nampula and Nacala in the north and a correspondence program.

The National Baptist Convention has an evening Bible school in Beira with 30 students.

The Assemblies of God church runs a Portuguese-language Bible school with 70 full-time and 160 part-time students and a Changana-language Bible school with 70 students, both in Maputo.

Other organizations train Christians through correspondence courses. Emmaus Bible School, operating as a wing of Nova Alianca Church, is a leader in this field. Their courses range from simple Bible studies to advanced courses in Portuguese. Studies are available in Sena, Shona, Chewa and Changana.

The Global Literature Lifeline seeks to train pastors through correspondence courses. Gospel Recordings is playing a vital role in reaching illiterate people through cassettes and phonettes. They have recordings in 16 languages and dialects.

NEEDS IN MOZAMBIQUE

• Mozambique's greatest need is for peace so that people may return with dignity to their fields and produce their own food, reestablish education and medical care, and freely carry the gospel throughout the country.

- Christian workers need leadership training through formal education, extension programs and correspondence courses. Basic literacy courses may be a necessary prerequisite.
- Emergency relief aid in the form of food, clothing, seed and medical supplies is desperately needed. Aid dependency, however, creates a loss of dignity, and must be avoided. Existing Mozambican assistance channels should be used where possible, and aid given that encourages people to help themselves. Programs should be coordinated to avoid duplicating effort and resources. Donors should avoid large gifts that could create divisions between church groups unable to receive similar quantities of the same kinds of goods.
- Christian workers and mission groups have many open doors to be involved in appropriate development programs. Small-scale agricultural and educational projects can be developed through local churches. Mission groups could work with churches to develop and staff refugee centers. Mission groups could also develop skill-training programs to equip local church members in self-sufficiency.
- Christian "tentmakers" also have many doors open. Jobs are available through the government or international agencies that allow a dedicated Christian to serve in the name of Jesus. Because of the current openness, there are few restrictions on direct Christian ministry and witness by such tentmakers.
- There is a great need to develop and distribute appropriate Christian literature material, including Sunday school material, training manuals and Bible study tools. There also is a tremendous need for Bibles and hymnbooks.
- Christian workers are needed to help in the enormous task of rebuilding Mozambique, but such people must be humble and willing to serve under the national church. They should be willing to adopt appropriate lifestyles that will not clash with the living standards of the local people.

BIBLIOGRAPHY

Africa Institute, *Africa Research Bulletin*, Bi-monthly briefings.

Europa Publishers, *Africa South of the Sahara 1989*.

American University, *Area Handbook for Mozambique*.

Barrett, David, *World Christian Encyclopedia*, Oxford University Press.

Economist, *EIU Country Report*, 1990/91.

Economist, *EIU Quarterly Report*, January 1991

Fletcher, Pascal, "Foreign Aid Can't Halt Mozambique Crisis," *Citizen*, March 31, 1989.

Government of the People's Republic of Mozambique and United Nations, *The Emergency Situation in Mozambique: Priority Requirements for the Period 1988-1989*.

Gersony, Robert, *Summary of Mozambican Refugee Accounts of Principally Conflict-Related Experience in Mozambique*, U.S. Department of State, April 1988.

Hallet A E, *Report on Christian Work*, May 1985.

Hanlon, Joseph, *Mozambique: The Revolution Under Fire*, London, Zed Books, 1984.

Isaacman, Allen and Barbara, *Mozambique: From Colonialism to Revolution*, Harare, Zimbabwe Publishing House, 1983.

Meiring, Piet, *Afrika: Die Hamer, Die Kruis en Die Sekel*, De Jager-Haum.

Refugees (United Nations, July-August 1988, pages 16-39): Bollag, Burton, "Destabilization: The Human Cost," Brouwer, Marjolein, "Children in Trauma," Chichini, Malak et al, "Four Crowded Camps," Crisp, Jeff, "Stretched to the Limit," "Flight from Violence, A Future in Ruvuma," Jacob, Sol, "Churches Minister to Mozambicans," Phillips, Jackson, "Running Out of Space, A Problem of Protection."

United States Committee for Refugees, *Shattered Land, Fragile Asylum: Refugees from Mozambique*, November 1986.

United States Department of State, *Background Notes*, May 1985.

United Bible Society, *World Annual Reports 1986 - 1987*.

Wycliffe Bible Translators, *Ethnologue: Eleventh Edition*.

RÉUNION

Co-edited by Michael Brooks

Profile

Natural features: Réunion is an oval-shaped island 700 km (437 miles) east of Madagascar in the Indian Ocean. The island has a land area of 2,512 km^2 (970 square miles), and is 209 km (130 square miles) in circumference. The island consists of two volcanic mountain ranges and a coastal plain. Some mountain peaks rise to 3,000 meters (10,000 feet).

Climate: The island is in the cyclonic belt, and rainfall averages 4,714 mm (1,855 square inches) a year in the uplands and 686 mm (270 square inches) at sea level. Average temperature for May to November is 25°C (78°F) with little rain. December to April is hot and wet and the average temperature is 30°C (86°F). It can be considerably cooler in the mountains.

Population: 578,500 (1989 estimate). Annual growth rate: 1.8%. Density: 227 per km^2 (596 per square mile) (1988). Population in the under-20 age group: 48%.

Ethnic groups: The majority of islanders are of mixed race, and their ethnic origins may be European, Asian and/or African. Some 26,000 people are French metropolitans (4.5%). Chinese, Indian, Comorian and Malagache peoples also live in Réunion.

Languages and literacy: 80% speak Creole as their home language. French is used in all official communication, newspapers, radio, television and schools and government. Some speak other languages in addition to French and Creole, including Tamil, Gujarati, Malagache and Chinese. Forty-nine percent of adult Creoles are illiterate.

Urbanization: (1982 census) St. Denis (capital), 109,068; St. Paul, 58,410; St. Pierre 50,081.

Government: Réunion was made a French *departement* in 1946. The island is administered by a General Council and a Regional Council. Four districts are divided into 24 municipalities. The current commissioner is Jean Anciaux. Réunion administers the small uninhabited islands of Bassas da India, Juan de Nova, Europa, Iles Glorieuses and Tromelin.

Economy: Currency: French francs; Ff5.1 = US$1 GDP: Ff16,337m (85). GDP per capita: Ff21,554. Trade: Imports: ('86) Ff7,861m; Exports: Ff945m. Inflation: 2.8% in 1987. Agriculture as % of GDP in 1982, 5%. Population employed in agriculture: 11.5% in 1985. Growth rate: 9.6% in 1987. Only 37% of the economically active population were employed in 1987.

Religion: Roman Catholic, 90.5%; Hindu, 7%; Protestant, 4.5%; Muslim, 4%; no religion, 3.5%; Baha'i, 1%; Christian sects, 0.5%;

HISTORICAL BACKGROUND

Although Réunion was uninhabited until the middle of the 17th century, Arabs, Dutch, Portuguese, English and French all knew of its existence.

The island was first called Grande Mascareigne, after a Portuguese navigator. When the French occupied the island in 1649, they named it Bourbon Island. The island became Réunion in 1793. In 1810, it was captured briefly by the British during the Napoleonic wars, and they renamed it Bourbon. The name of the island reverted to Réunion in 1848.

Réunion was governed as a colony until 1946 when it was granted the status of a French *departement*. French subsidies provide assistance during unemployment and other social benefits. In 1978, when the Organization for African Unity called for independence for the island, few people in Réunion actually wanted independence.

THE PEOPLE

Intermarriage and customary unions have blurred the ethnic origins of the majority of the people in Réunion. Most of the people are Creole. About 23 percent of the population are recognizably of European descent. Of this figure, 26,000 are metropolitan French. Not all of these are in the upper class.

Hindus

About 120,000 people are Tamil-speaking Hindus. Of these, 90,000 describe themselves as Indian in origin. They were brought to the island to serve as indentured labor for the sugar farms, and now live mainly on the eastern side of the island.

Although a large percent of these people profess to be Catholic, they practice Hindu rites. Practicing Hindus are trying to bring these "Catholic Hindus" back into the fold, and Swamis have been brought from India to teach true Hindu religion. The Hindus publish a review called *Sakthi*, and have requested time on the national radio and television transmissions.

Muslims

The majority of the 15,000 Muslims in Réunion are Gujarati and Sunni by tradition. These people have retained their ethnic identity. In addition to the Muslims of Indian origin, about 1,000 from Madagascar are Shia by tradition. Some 5,000 Comorian Muslims are included in the total of 15,000. A number of Creole people are turning to Islam.

Muslims are represented by an association called *Islam Surtee Sunnate Djamate*. All the major towns have mosques. St. Denis has several prayer houses in addition to two mosques. Koranic schools for children are held at each mosque. The Islamic community publishes a bi-weekly newssheet called *Al Islam*.

Chinese

Twenty thousand people of Chinese origin live in Réunion. Chinese immigration began in 1844, when Hakka-speaking contract workers were brought into the country. Later, independent traders arrived who were mainly Cantonese-speaking.

The majority of Chinese profess to be Catholic. Because the older generation still retain their Buddhist ties, however, and respect is paid to wishes of elders, religion is dualistic. Babies are baptized as Catholics but Buddhist rites are still practiced.

The majority of Chinese people are involved in commerce and retail trade. No evangelical church is specifically reaching Chinese people.

SOCIOECONOMIC CONDITIONS

The economy of Réunion is fairly advanced. France is its main trading partner, providing 67 percent of its imports and consuming 73 percent of its exports in 1973. Réunion's status as a *département* of France ensures heavy French subsidization of social programs and wage structures.

Unemployment is a problem. In 1987, about 80,000 people were unemployed. Most people without jobs were under 25 years of age. Many emigrate to France in search of work.

Education

Education is based on the French system, and is compulsory for children between six and 16 years old. Study is in French. This causes problems, particularly for Creole children, who are not comfortable speaking French. Some 49 percent of adult Creoles are illiterate. Many adults have had little or no primary education.

Agriculture

Dense forests once covered most of the island, but today, only 35 percent of the island is forested. Some 26 percent of the land is arable, of which nearly half is used to cultivate sugar, the island's main crop. More recently, the country is trying to move away from sugar production, and small farmers are being encouraged to plant fruit and market gardens. This has provided employment for more than 2,500 farmers.

Health

Réunion has 19 doctors and a medical center in each borough. Most of the doctors operate under the National Health Service.

Table 1: SOCIAL INDICATORS IN BRIEF

Total enrollment in schools (excluding pre-primary)	146,825
Enrollment in primary schools	51%
Enrollment in secondary schools	47%
Enrollment in tertiary education	2%
Adult literacy rate	51%
Population per doctor	1,260
Population under 20 years	60%

STATUS OF CHRISTIANITY

Visiting priests ministered to early French settlers on the island. The first mass on the island was celebrated in 1655, and a congregation was established in 1666 at St. Paul. Lazarites were the first resident priests to arrive on the island.

It was many years before Protestants arrived. Seventh Day Adventists spearheaded the way, enduring threats, persecution and discrimination at the hands of the Catholic community.

Today, freedom of religion is guaranteed under the French constitution. Ninety percent of the people profess membership in the Roman Catholic Church. The number of people who practice their faith, however, is substantially less.

Protestant Christianity is increasing rapidly. Most of the Protestant community is evangelical, but their numbers are small. They number about 4.5 percent of the population.

The accommodating attitude towards Protestantism in the Vatican II decisions made a big difference to Protestant witness in Réunion. For the first time, people were allowed to own a Bible.

Since then, many have become more responsive to the Christian message. Some are joining the renewal movement within the Catholic church. The Assemblies of God is growing quickly as members seek to heal and deliver people from the spirit world.

This hunger for truth and freedom has led some to turn elsewhere for answers. Muslims report that people of the island are turning to Islam because they are disillusioned with the emptiness of their own religion.

Table 2: RELIGIOUS AFFILIATION IN RÉUNION

Roman Catholic Church	463,035 (est.)
Assemblies of God	20,000
Seventh Day Adventists	3,000
Evangelical Church	800
Other Protestant groups	1,500 (est.)

NATIONAL CHURCHES

Roman Catholic Church

In 1711, Pope Clement entrusted the evangelization of Réunion to the Lazarites. Other groups arrived in later years. One of the larger groups is *Freres des Ecoles Chretiennes*, who arrived in 1817, and now have 34 members in six communities.

Today, a single diocese with nine districts is responsible directly to the Holy See. Nine congregations on the island, both religious and secular, involve 96 priests, of whom 33 are Réunionnais. The ratio of more than 4,800 church members to one priest is high, contributing to extensive syncretism and nominalism in the church.

Thirteen congregations of women are involved in ministry on the island. Of 405 sisters, 335 are Réunionnais. The largest of these congregations is *Congrégation des Filles de Marie* and *Congrégation des Soeurs de St-Joseph de Cluny*.

The church runs a hospital, 23 primary schools, 10 secondary and technical schools and an agricultural college.

There is a strong renewal movement in the Réunion Roman Catholic Church. Rather than regard it as sectarian, the Catholic church seeks to bring the renewal movement into the whole denomination.

The church is concerned about the 80,000 Tamil Indian Catholics, many of whom also practice Hindu rituals, and is seeking to be more relevant to their needs.

The church also serves the people of Comores. Two priests, one of whom is on Mayotte, minister to the islands, and two sisters work in health care.

Protestant churches

ASSEMBLIES OF GOD
(ASSEMBLÉES DE DIEU DE LA RÉUNION)

The Assemblies of God denomination in Réunion is also known as *Mission Salut et Guérison*. Aimé Cizeron began the work in 1966. The early years were difficult, and they were initially regarded as a cult. Nevertheless, the church has grown rapidly. Today, 20,000 active members worship at 30 churches and 100 preaching points.

The church believes in equipping the laity through "hands-on" training. Leadership schools are held twice a year for pastors.

EVANGELICAL CHURCH
(L'EGLISE EVANGELIQUE DE LA RÉUNION)

Africa Evangelical Fellowship began a ministry on the island in 1971, and established a church in 1974. Today, the Evangelical Church in Réunion is made up of eight autonomous churches, each separately registered with the government. About 800 members worship at these churches.

While a number of missions support these developing churches, leadership is in the hands of national committees. A Union of Evangelical Churches is being formed to coordinate work and stimulate growth.

SEVENTH DAY ADVENTISTS

Seventh Day Adventists first entered the country in 1936. Their early efforts were accompanied by great difficulties and threats of persecution. They persevered, however, and today have 15 churches with 1,100 members as well as several thousand adherents and children. Their churches are continuing to grow, but the materialistic influence of France is a deterrent. Those seeking training are sent to France or Rwanda.

Other small Protestant churches include:

- Reformed Church (*Eglise Réforméde le Réunion*), with a church in St. Denis
- Gospel Bible Church
- Pentecostal Church
- Christian Centre
- Jesus Saves (Unitarian)

FOREIGN MISSIONARIES

Few Protestant foreign missionaries work in Réunion. Africa Evangelical Fellowship was the first missionary society to begin a ministry there, and the Evangelical church grew out of their work.

Other missions assisting the Evangelical church include the Africa Inland Mission and the Swiss Evangelical Mission.

Youth with a Mission (YWAM) has recently started work in the St. Pierre area. They plan to start a discipleship training school.

UNREACHED PEOPLES

Many on Réunion have never clearly understood Christ's offer of salvation, despite their membership in a Christian church. This is particularly true of people who practice the Malabar religion, a syncretistic form of Hinduism mixed with Catholicism and African witchcraft. Some 48 percent of the population practice the Malabar religion. They see Catholic rituals, such as baptism, confirmation and the sacraments, as their external religion but do not rely on Catholicism to deal with daily problems caused by spirit activity and culture. These needs are met though the Malabar religion.

Special initiatives are necessary to reach the 40,000 Hindus and 20,000 Muslims.

About 20,000 Metropolitan French are generally indifferent or atheistic and have no church connections.

Transcendental Meditation followers have two centers in St. Denis. About 5,000 Baha'i are active on the island, and about 1,000 Mormons and 1,665 Jehovah's Witnesses in 19 localities live in Réunion.

CHRISTIAN ACTIVITIES

Evangelism

Twenty years ago, few evangelical Christians lived in Réunion, but today the number is increasing steadily. The Assemblies of God has a "Decade of Harvest" planned to reach many people on the island for Christ. The Evangelical church is steadily working among the many nominal and syncretistic people who need to hear the message of salvation. Radio programs and literature ministry are helping to reach people.

Broadcasting

There are few restrictions on private radio transmitters. The Roman Catholic Church owns private radio stations, broadcasting 11 hours daily. Seventh Day Adventists and the Assemblies of God church at St. Paul also run stations.

The Roman Catholic Church also broadcasts one hour each week on the national radio service, and Seventh Day Adventists have a 10-minute program on the national service each Sunday.

FEBA radio, broadcasting from Seychelles, is transmitted on shortwave and receives many interested responses from Réunion.

Literature

The work of the Bible Society is conducted from Mauritius. The Evangelical church has a bookshop in St. Denis. The Roman Catholic church has a *Centre de Documentation* in St. Denis. A number of small libraries operate at parish level.

The Seventh Day Adventists operate a bookshop in St. Denis.

Magazines are published by the Roman Catholic Church (bi-monthly), the Seventh Day Adventists (three times a year), and the Assemblies of God (quarterly).

Christian education

The Roman Catholic Church has a seminary that has recently been reopened after being closed for a number of years. Seven seminarians are in training on the island, and their training will be completed in France. The seminary also includes training for sisters and lay workers. Currently, 400 lay workers are in training as catechists. They spend each weekend training over a period of two years, and two months of full-time training each year. Over 3,000 catechists have also been trained at this center.

A Bible School, CIFEM, is a ministry of St. Pierre Evangelical Church, but is not currently training any Réunionnais.

The Assemblies of God trains lay people to reach out to others on the island and beyond.

Social work

The French government pays unemployment and social benefits so there is little economic need on the island that can be met by the church. Ministry to families is of concern to the church and a number of centers seek to minister in this area. Alcoholism, generally associated with unemployment, is a problem.

NEEDS IN RÉUNION

- Leadership training is a vital need in Réunion.
- Evangelical church leaders want training in Muslim evangelism.
- Chinese people, who go through the motions of the Catholic faith but practice Buddhism, need deliverance from the bondage of ancestral worship and tradition.
- Syncretistic Malabar people have never really understood what it means to be Christian. They need to know that Christ offers freedom from the Hindu spirit world.
- The materialistic influence of France is great. Discipleship training on the cost of commitment for new Christians is essential.

BIBLIOGRAPHY

Aubrey, Mnsr. Gilbert, *Pour Dieu et pour l'Homme Réunionnais*, Ocean Editions 1980.

Baptiste, Pere Emile, *St. Andre Ma Paroisse*, 1989.

Bullier, Antoine J, "Réunion: French foothold?" *Africa Institute Bulletin* No. 2, 1983.

Foulon, Alain, *Religions a la Réunion*, Medias Creations, 1989.

REPUBLIC OF SEYCHELLES

Co-edited by James Sabadin

Profile

Natural features: The Seychelles archipelago consists of 115 islands scattered over an economic zone of more than 1,000,000 km^2 (400 square miles) of the Indian Ocean. The estimated land area is 443 km^2 (175 square miles). The majority of the islands are coralline while 41 are granite. Mahé, the largest island, lies 1,800 km. (1,000 miles) east of Mombassa, Kenya on the African coast and is situated 4° south of the equator. The second largest island is Praslin, 21 miles (34 km) to the northeast.

Climate: Tropical with two seasons; hot from December to May, with high humidity, and cooler from June to November. The average annual rainfall in Mahé is 2,360 mm (93 inches) and the average temperature is 27°C (80°F). The granite islands, including Mahé and Praslin, lie outside the cyclone belt.

Population: 68,000 (estimate for 1990). Eighty percent of the population lives on Mahé. The coral islands are largely uninhabited. Annual growth rate is 0.6% when emigration is taken into account. Population density: 207 per km^2 (536 per square mile).

Languages and literacy: English, Creole and French are official languages but Creole is the *lingua franca*. English is the language of administration.

Urbanization: Victoria, on the island of Mahé, is the largest town with an estimated population of 23,000.

Government: A one-party republic. The People's Assembly consists of 23 members elected by adult suffrage. The head of state is President France Albert René, who is also Minister of Defense, Environment, Industry and Legal Affairs.

Economy: Currency: 100 cents = 1 Seychelles rupee. Exchange rate: Average for 1990 was SR5.393 = US$1. GDP (1988): SR1,745 million. GDP per capita: SR25,661 (US$4,758). Growth rate: 4% (1990). Imports: US$1,529 m (1988). Exports: US$13.7 m. Origins of GDP: Agriculture and fishing, 5%; tourism, 11%; labor force in agriculture, 18%; inflation rate, 6% in 1990.

Religion: Roman Catholic, 87%; Anglican 7.5%; other Protestant, 2%; sects and non-Christian religions, 3.5%.

HISTORICAL BACKGROUND

Before the French arrived, the islands of Seychelles were uninhabited. Although a number of navigators visited the islands, settlement did not begin until the French arrived in 1770. Their mandate was to set up administration and supply food for passing ships. Because Seychelles-based privateers marauded ships heading eastward, the British captured the settlement in 1774.

Control of Seychelles alternated between the British and the French until the British finally occupied the islands.

In 1810, Seychelles became a British dependency and in 1903, a British Crown Colony. Despite British control, the Seychellois retained more French influence than English.

In 1830, an Anglican missionary reported that there were 8,000 people on the islands, of whom 6,000 were slaves. When the British emancipated the slaves, a number of landowners left the island with their slaves, and the population fell to less than 4,500 in 1840. The islands soon became a home for freed slaves, however, and the population began to grow rapidly.

After 1970, several movements towards self-government led to independence in June 1976. Seychelles became an independent republic within the Commonwealth, with James Mancham as the first president of a coalition government.

In June 1977, a *coup d'etat* was declared and Albert René was sworn in as president. He introduced a socialist one-party political system with the result that his administration has not been openly or officially opposed.

René's government has adopted a non-aligned policy and has good relations with the west. Ties with the Soviet Union and countries such as Libya, Algeria, and Iraq also have been strengthened. The islands are strategically placed, and René has secured aid from superpowers in exchange for the placement of a US tracking station and the servicing of USSR warships.

SOCIOECONOMIC CONDITIONS

The country's income per capita is US$4,758 a year, which places Seychelles in the upper middle income bracket. State and para-statal companies account for half the country's national income and two-thirds of employment, but the government gradually is relaxing its hold on the economy.

Seychelles has a high unemployment rate but it also has a shortage of professionals. The government is concerned about the emigration of qualified Seychellois.

Tourism is the mainstay of Seychelles' economy, but the government has tried to reduce dependence on this source of income.

Health

Private health services have been phased out, leaving the government responsible for health services. More health funding has helped reduce infectious diseases and the infant mortality rate, and also helped raise life expectancy. Seychelles is free of many tropical diseases, including malaria and bilharzia. The island depends on expatriate doctors.

Education

Education is also controlled by the government. Church schools were taken over by the government at independence. Today, education is free and compulsory for children aged six to 15 years. By 1986, one-third of the population was attending school, including preschool crèches.

The first few years of schooling is in Creole, after which most of the teaching is in English. Creole is then taught in language courses, as is French. Two years of National Youth Service follows, and then a polytechnic provides technical courses and A-level tuition in the British education system. There are 25 primary schools and two secondary schools in Seychelles.

Agriculture

Some 10 percent of the land is arable, but agricultural production is insignificant. The fishing industry is expanding.

Table 1: SOCIAL INDICATORS IN BRIEF

Total enrollment in schools (excluding preschool)	18,637
Enrollment in primary schools	78%
Enrollment in secondary schools	13%
Enrollment in tertiary education (excluding those abroad)	8.2%
Pupil/teacher ratio	20:3
Literacy rate	85%
Population per doctor	985
Population per hospital bed	200
Population per nurse	251
Infant mortality rate per 1,000	18.4
Population growth rate (with emigration)	0.6%
Life expectancy	69 years

THE PEOPLE

After emancipation, Seychelles became a place for freed slaves. Because of the high degree of intermarriage and customary unions, the government was not able to make distinctions between different ethnic groups in the 1901 census. Today, the people regard themselves as Creole, and a common language binds them together.

Most of the Indian population trace their roots to an immigration of merchants in the 1880s and 1890s. A minority of Indians from Bombay and Gujarat have retained their ethnic uniqueness and cultural identity. The Indian population are mostly involved in trade.

The first Chinese also arrived from Mauritius during this period. Later, groups of immigrant Chinese traders arrived from Canton. Some Chinese have also retained strong ethnic identity. The majority of Chinese are retailers.

There is little formal class distinction in Seychelles, although a higher informal status often is given to those with lighter skin.

Because of the high rate of customary unions, or *en menage*, families are called "domestic groups." In 1971, 45 percent of children were born to unmarried parents. By 1980, this number had jumped to 64 percent. Today, it is estimated that 70 percent of children are born out of wedlock.

STATUS OF CHRISTIANITY

Seychelles is overwhelmingly Catholic, with aproximately 87 percent of the population claiming allegiance to the Roman Catholic Church. Protestants, including Anglicans, number nearly 8 percent.

Table 2: ESTIMATED RELIGIOUS AFFILIATION

Roman Catholics	59,000
Anglicans	5,000
Seventh Day Adventists	500
Pentecostal Assembly	500
Other Protestant groups	300
Hindus	1,000
Baha'i	500
Muslims	300
Jehovah's Witnesses	75

Although most of the people attend church regularly, and are baptized and confirmed, witchcraft or superstition (*gris-gris*) is widespread. Some Seychellois see no contradiction between Christianity and magic. Until recently, it was common practice to baptize a baby in the church and then take the baby to the witch doctor for protection rites.

Churches are challenging this duality, and the number of people who renounce witchcraft and superstition to follow Christ is growing. Renewal is beginning to have an impact in the Anglican church also. About 2 percent of the population have made a wholehearted commitment to Jesus Christ, renouncing all witchcraft, superstitious rites, and magic.

NATIONAL CHURCHES

Roman Catholic Church

The earliest record of Christian witness in Seychelles was a Roman Catholic chapel that was established by the French Catholics who arrived in the late 18th century. Catholicism continued to grow despite the fact that British authorities forbade any Catholic priest from living on the island. Finally, in 1850, a Capuchin priest was allowed to arrive, and established three more churches. Nuns from the Congregation of Sisters arrived in 1861.

Today there are 17 Catholic churches, with 14 on the island of Mahé. Chapels on some of the smaller islands are tended by visiting priests. Twelve religious and secular priests, four of whom are Seychellois, care for the large Catholic population, in a ratio of more than 5,500 members per priest.

Saint Joseph of Cluny, with 36 sisters, constitutes the largest religious order. Other orders working in Seychelles are St. Elizabeth's, Missionaries of Charity, and Sisters la Providence.

There are no training facilities on the island. Those seeking to train as priests or sisters need to travel to Réunion, Madagascar or France.

The church makes up a single diocese responsible directly to the Holy See. Mgr. Félix Paul, a Seychellois, is the bishop of the diocese. The church runs an orphanage in Victoria.

Anglican church

In 1830, the Society for the Propagation of the Gospel (SPG) sent a missionary to Seychelles. Although he intended only to make a report, he decided to stay. Within a year of his arrival he had baptized 500 nominal Catholics. Another visiting clergyman baptized 543 people in 1840.

The first minister to settle on the islands, Rev. George Delafontaine, arrived in 1843. During his 10 years of ministry, the number of baptized Anglicans rose to more than 2,400. Their status as Anglicans was short-lived, however, since a Capuchin friar re-baptized them all as Catholics.

At first, the Anglican church grew haphazardly because clergy visits were sporadic and the church did not maintain a continuous presence.

In 1855, the Right Reverend Ryan was consecrated the first Bishop of Mauritius and Seychelles. The following year the first church in Seychelles was consecrated at Praslin. Today the church is stronger numerically in Praslin than anywhere else.

St. Paul's Cathedral became a pro Cathedral in 1930, and was raised to Cathedral status in 1960. It became an independent Cathedral in 1973, when the Province of the Indian Ocean was formed and Seychelles became a separate diocese from Mauritius with its own resident bishop.

In 1963, the Reverend French Chang-Him was ordained as the first Seychellois Anglican priest. He became the spiritual leader of the church in 1979 when he was installed as Bishop of Seychelles, and later as Archbishop of the Church of the Province of the Indian Ocean.

Today, 11 churches form a single diocese in Seychelles. With an estimated 5,000 members, the church constitutes only 7.5 percent of the total population, compared with 14 percent in 1901. In 1987, approximately 600 church members attended church regularly.

The Anglican church faces the challenge of developing church growth programs to bring nominal members into active fellowship.

Protestant churches

SEVENTH DAY ADVENTISTS

In 1930, the director of the Mauritian Seventh Day Adventist mission and an evangelist arrived to work in Seychelles. Permission was granted by the Governor to hold meetings. After six years of struggle and opposition, the 50 people who had become members built a church in Victoria. In 1940, they started a school that continued to teach children until it was handed over to the government in 1979.

The church has continued to grow, and today 350 adult members and an equal number of children attend. There are three organized churches in Mahé and one at Praslin without a resident pastor.

Open public gatherings are prohibited in Seychelles, and revival meetings are carried out within the church walls. Evangelical outreach is limited to home visitation and prayer groups known as evangelical units. A welfare organization called Dorcas serves the needy.

Pentecostal churches

PENTECOSTAL ASSEMBLY OF SEYCHELLES

In 1981, a prayer group met in the home of a woman with a deep desire to win people for Christ. The group grew rapidly and sought help from the Pentecostal Assemblies of Canada. In 1985, a missionary arrived to help.

The church has grown rapidly on Mahé, challenging people with the need for repentance and a new way of life. The church plans to establish home groups in 20 districts that will eventually become autonomous churches. To achieve this goal, people are being trained on different levels, from simple discipleship courses to advanced training. A cassette ministry forms part of their ministry and training program, and includes Scripture on tape.

Four hundred fifty members and a hundred children gather for worship each week. A new building is under construction to accommodate the growing congregation.

Several smaller church groups gather to worship, including Full Gospel Church of God, Grace and Peace Fellowship, and Jesus Only.

UNREACHED PEOPLES

Hinduism was brought to Seychelles by Indian traders. Some Hindus have intermarried and become Catholics, but many Indians have retained their ethnic and religious identity. A Hindu temple is being built in Victoria.

There are 300 Muslims in Seychelles. A mosque in Victoria serves the Muslim community, and their children are trained at a Koranic school. Although Islam was introduced by Indian merchants, the majority of adherents are now Seychellois.

Baha'i have been active on the islands and people worship in 20 localities. Although the Baha'i church claims to have many adherents, others estimate that there are only 500 practicing members. They distribute literature from their center in Victoria.

FOREIGN MISSIONARIES

Few expatriates work in Seychelles and visas for missionary work are difficult to obtain. Protestant agencies include the Africa Inland Mission, the Pentecostal Assemblies of Canada, and the United Society for the Propagation of the Gospel.

All the missionaries working in Seychelles were either invited by existing local denominations or came to work in professional capacities.

FEBA has a radio station in Seychelles that transmits programs in 28 languages to more than 30 countries. No programs are prepared for, or specifically broadcast to Seychelles. FEBA missionaries are not formally involved in ministry to the islanders.

CHRISTIAN ACTIVITIES

Evangelism

In 1977, when the strongly socialist government gained control, the church was restricted in a number of ways. Today, the church in Seychelles is free to evangelize, but meetings may only be held inside church buildings.

Staying within this restriction, the Anglican church has programs aimed at renewal and growth, and the Pentecostal church's "Decade of Destiny" has goals to reach nominal and syncretistic Christians with the message of salvation.

Broadcasting

About 16,000 radios were used in Seychelles in 1987. The Catholic church has a radio studio that prepares programs for transmission on the national service.

One hour each Sunday is allotted for a church service. This time is shared by the Catholic church and the Anglican church. An additional 15 minutes each week is shared by these two churches in ministry to families. The Seventh Day Adventists and the Baha'i also share a weekly slot.

Although FEBA does not aim to reach Seychellois people, it is possible to pick up their transmission in English and French.

Literature

Most Seychellois are not avid readers. Since Creole has only recently become a written language, literacy is low. It is anticipated, however, that this will change now that education is compulsory.

The majority of educated people prefer to read English instead of Creole, but the production of literature in Creole is nevertheless necessary as more of the population learns to read. The Christian Resource Center, a ministry of the Anglican church, is seeking to meet the need by providing Creole literature, particularly for children, and a number of books for children are currently being translated and printed. A Creole orthography is still in process.

The Bible Society has established an office in Seychelles. The Gospel of Luke in Creole has been published and the Gospel of Mark is on the press. The translation of the New Testament is now complete and will be published with Psalms in a joint venture by Anglicans, Seventh Day Adventists and Roman Catholics. The Gospel of Mark will also be available on cassette. Easy reading selections are available in three booklets.

The Anglican church has a bookshop. The Catholic church has a printing works and bookshop.

The Roman Catholic Church publishes a fortnightly magazine called *L'Echo des Iles* and the Anglicans produce a quarterly called *Diocesan Magazine Seychelles.*

Education

In the early years of settlement, the Anglican church and later the Catholic church established schools. The Seventh Day Adventists had one school.

The colonial government did not become involved in education until 1947. The government granted subsidies, but the schools remained under church control. At independence, the education system was nationalized and mission schools passed to state control.

Seychelles is so small that the church is unable to sustain full-time Christian training centers. As a result, training for ministry usually takes place in other countries.

In 1987, however, the Anglican church established a training center, St. Phillips, and four trainees have graduated after four years of training. In future years, the center will become a conference center for the Province of the Indian Ocean but will continue to train people full-time as the need arises.

The Pentecostal church is training lay leaders through the ministries of the church, using International Correspondence Institute materials.

NEEDS IN SEYCHELLES

- Despite the fact that 96.5 percent of the population claim to belong to a Christian church, their lives are full of fear and superstition. Many still need to hear about God's salvation from the powers of darkness.

- Catholic Seychellois who experience renewal and new life in Christ need support whether they decide to stay in the Catholic church or join another Christian group. Those who want to leave face a great deal of family pressure and even ostracism.

- One of the greatest social problems facing the church in Seychelles is the system of customary unions and the high level of illegitimacy. Family relationships are so complex and the immoral practice of *en menage* so deeply entrenched that there is no easy answer to ethical and moral problems. Compounding the difficulties are health problems related to sexually-transmitted diseases.

- Alcohol consumption is increasing rapidly, as is unemployment and drug abuse among young people.
- Although jobs are difficult to find, there are openings for trained and skilled professionals that could be filled by Seychellois who return to their island after being trained or by expatriate "tentmakers."

BIBLIOGRAPHY

EIU Country Profile, 1990/91.

EIU Quarterly Reports, January 1991.

Emmanuel, The Ven. G., *Diocese of Mauritius*, 1810 - 1841.

Franda, Marcus, *The Seychelles, Unquiet Islands*, Westview Press, 1982.

Huntley, David, *Seychelles Christians, Yesterday Today, Tomorrow*, an assignment for Fuller School of World Mission, 1987.

The Seventh Day Adventist Mission in Seychelles, *Seychelles: 50 Years, A Review of Events*.

Thomas, Athol, *Forgotten Eden*, Longman, 1968.

ST HELENA with ASCENSION and TRISTAN da CUNHA

Co-edited by Rob Lennox

Profile

Natural features: St. Helena is an 122km^2 (47 square miles) island nearly 2,000 kilometers (1,250 miles) southwest of Africa in the South Atlantic Ocean. The island is volcanic in origin and its highest elevation is 828 meters (2,716 feet).

Climate: Mild, with temperatures ranging from 21-29°C (65- 82°F) in summer to 18-23°C (62-67°F) in winter. Rainfall ranges from 188 mm (7inches) in Jamestown to 1,039 mm (42inches) in the east.

Population: 5,559 (1987 census). Population increased by 7.4% since the previous census in 1976. Population density: 45 per kilometer (118 per square mile).

Ethnic groups: Some 98% of the population are St. Helenans, a mixed-race group with African, Asian, European and Polynesian origins. The rest are citizens of the United Kingdom or other European countries.

Languages and literacy: The most common language spoken in St. Helena is English. Adult literacy rate is 100%.

Government: St. Helena is a crown colony of the United Kingdom. The governor, R.F. Stimson, is also responsible for the islands of Ascension and Tristan da Cunha. The constitution allows for a Legislative Council, an Executive Council and Council Committees. Jamestown is the capital.

Economy: 100 pence = £1 St. Helena, which is on a par with U.K. pound. Inflation rate: 15% over the period 1983-1986. Imports (1984): £3,219,960. Exports (1985): £24,744.

Religion: Anglican 91%; Protestant 6%; Roman Catholic 1.5%; Jehovah's Witnesses 1.5%.

HISTORICAL BACKGROUND

The island of St. Helena was discovered by a Portuguese navigator in 1502. It remained uninhabited until 1659, when the British East India Company established a settlement. St. Helena drew international attention when Napoleon Bonaparte was exiled on the island in 1815 and stayed there until his death five years later. The island was brought under the British crown in 1834.

In 1983, a commission reviewed the present constitution and found that the majority of islanders were unwilling to make any changes.

SOCIOECONOMIC CONDITIONS

St. Helena depends heavily on financial aid from Britain to meet its budget, and as a result, life is economically secure. The crime rate is low, and there are few accidental deaths. The government provides for the people through a national health program, pensions, subsidized foods and employment.

Although most of the island's food is imported, its economy is based on agriculture. The main crops are maize and potatoes. Land for agriculture is available on a rental basis or leasehold. A forestry program provides the island's timber needs. Fisheries provide employment and adequate fish for local consumption and export.

The government creates job opportunities for some while others find work on the island of Ascension. Jobs there provide resources for families of contract workers. On Ascension, people are exposed to a more materialistic way of life. Often, their value systems change as a result.

Lack of housing is a problem for young people who wish to marry. The alternatives are to live with parents or delay marriage, which encourages immorality.

Education is compulsory and free and operates on the British education system. A hospital in Jamestown employs three doctors, (British), a British matron and nursing sisters. Nurses who work in the hospital are locally trained.

Communication with most of the world is poor and there is no air-link. The nearest landing strip is on Ascension, two days' boat ride away. A shipping service operates six times a year between the United Kingdom, Ascension, St. Helena and Cape Town in South Africa.

NATIONAL CHURCHES

Although no organization links all of the denominations in St. Helena, ministers, pastors, and priests meet informally on a regular basis.

Roman Catholic Church

The Roman Catholic Church is a small community which fluctuates according to the expatriate staff on the island. The islands were cared for by the Archbishop of Cape Town until 1986, when the work was handed over to the Mill Hill Fathers. A permanent priest was installed in 1988.

Anglican church

The Anglican church (Church of the Province of Southern Africa) was the first to establish a church on the island, and today 91 percent of the island is nominally Anglican.

The church had its origins in early British settlement. In 1850, Bishop Gray visited St. Helena in order to encourage and strengthen the work. He ordained another deacon, bringing the number of clergy to four. The bishop was deeply concerned about the pitiful condition of the people on the island, who had been rescued from slave-ships.

In 1859, Dr. Piers Claughton was consecrated as the first Bishop of St. Helena. He set out to consolidate the work on the island. According to church records, there were 370 communicant members in 1875, but church adherents were estimated to number 4,200 more.

St. Helena is now a diocese of the Church of the Province of Southern Africa. Five clergy care for four parishes with 13 preaching points. The Diocese of St. Helena is also responsible for the only church on Ascension. Four of the present clergy have been sent from Britain by the Society for the Propagation of the Gospel.

Protestant churches

SALVATION ARMY

The Salvation Army has had a witness on the island since 1884. Three corps have approximately 100 members. They provide meals-on-wheels for shut-ins and a friendship club for senior citizens. The Salvation Army also produces a one-hour weekly radio program on the Government Broadcasting Service. A resthouse offers accommodation for the homeless. A campsite at Ross Rock is patronized by youth groups and others in the church.

BAPTIST CHURCH

The Baptist church began on the island in 1845, when Dr. James McGregor Bertram came to minister at the invitation of the Governor who had already begun a home Bible study. In 1899, the church became a member of the Baptist Union of Southern Africa, which sent pastors to minister on the island from 1960 1981. There are chapels at Jamestown, Knowlcombes, Sandy Bay and Headowain but the work is organized as one church. There are 60-70 members as well as a number of adherents.

ASCENSION

Portuguese discovered Ascension in 1501 but it was not inhabited until 1815, when a British garrison took occupation. It was made a dependency of St. Helena in 1922.

Ascension is a rocky volcanic island lying 1,131 km northwest of St. Helena and is 88 km^2 in area. It is an important communication center which provides international networking facilities. The population of 1,000 consists mainly of St. Helenans who have come to seek employment on the island. Expatriate communication contract workers make up the balance of the population. Most of the provisions needed are flown in from the United States, although some crops are grown for local consumption.

Status of Christianity

The Anglican church (Church of the Province of Southern Africa) is a parish of the island of St. Helena and has a resident priest. The church in St. Helena is in turn a diocese of the Church of the Province of Southern Africa. The majority of the migrant workers from St. Helena are Anglicans.

Visiting Roman Catholic priests have established a small Catholic work. About 200 to 300 Catholics live on the island, many of whom are expatriates, but few attend the occasional mass held on the island.

TRISTAN DA CUNHA

Tristan da Cunha is a volcanic island 2,400 km (1,500 miles) west of Cape Town. Britain took possession of the island in 1816, and in 1938 Tristan da Cunha was made a dependency of St. Helena. Contact with the outside world is limited to a vessel from South Africa that visits eight times a year, and a ship from St. Helena that visits once a year.

Land area is 98 km^2 (38 square miles), and the island is volcanic. An eruption in 1961 forced the evacuation of the island. Today, about 300 people live on the island, working for the fishing industry that exports its catch to the U.S.A, Japan and France.

STATUS OF CHRISTIANITY

The Anglican church began in 1816, when a British garrison was established on the island. A small church was founded and a building erected that also served as a school. Through the years, a few clergy who were willing to share the rigorous life of the settlers came to Tristan da Cunha. Today, most of the islanders are Anglican. The Church of the Province of Southern Africa has one church which falls under the jurisdiction of the Archdeacon of Mitchell's Plain in Cape Town.

A small number of Roman Catholics live on the island, but there is no resident priest.

NEEDS FOR THE ISLANDS

- Nominal Christians need to be challenged to experience a vital relationship with God.
- Special ministry is needed for contract labor workers on Ascension who are exposed to a modernized and materialistic life style on that island.
- Practical needs include housing, especially for young families, water purification, and job creation for unemployed.

BIBLIOGRAPHY

Barrett, David, *World Christian Encyclopedia*, Oxford University Press.

Brooke, Audrey, *Robert Gray*, Oxford University Press.

Europa Publications Limited, *Africa South of the Sahara 1989*.

Wirgman, A.T., *The History of the English Church and People in South Africa*, Longmans 1895.

Church and missions newsletters and periodicals.

REPUBLIC OF ZAMBIA

Co-edited by Joseph Imakando

Profile

Natural features: With 7,526,618 km^2 (290,586 square miles) of land, Zambia is a butterfly-shaped landlocked country sharing borders with eight countries. The terrain is mainly gentle undulating grasslands 900 to 1,500 meters (3,000 - 5,000 feet) above sea level. The Muchinga escarpment is in the northeast, and ranges about 2,000 m (6,560 feet). Swampland surrounds Lake Bangweulu.

Climate: Zambia has three distinct seasons: dry and cool from May to August, 13-27°C (53-80°F); hot and dry from September to October, 17-33°C (61-90°F); and hot and wet from November to April, 27-33°C (80-90°F). Rainfall ranges from 1,250 mm (49 inches) in the north to 500-750 mm (20-30 inches) in the south.

Population: 8,080,000 (1990 estimate). Population growth rate: 3.6% per year. Population density: 9.7 per km^2 (28 per square mile) in 1987. Rural population density: 4.3 per km^2.

Ethnic groups: 98% of the population belong to seven major ethnic groups: Bemba, Tonga, Nyanja, Lunda-Luvale, Barotse, Mambwe, and Tukumbe. There are between 30,000 and 40,000 Asians, and about 20,000 whites.

Languages and literacy: English is the official language, but 98% of the people speak one or more of the 80 different languages in Zambia. The main languages spoken are Bemba, Nyanja, Tonga, Lozi, Lunda, Luvale and Kaonde. Literacy rate: 59% (1988 estimate). Illiteracy is common in rural areas.

Urbanization: 54% (1988). The capital city is Lusaka, with 870,000 people in 1988. Other towns are Kitwe (472,000), Ndola (443,000), Mufulira (199,000), and Chingola (194,000). The country is divided into nine provinces. Urban growth rate: 7.4%.

Government: One-party state headed by President Dr. Kenneth Kaunda.

Economy: Currency: 100 Ngwee = K1; K30 = US$1 (Average 1990). K50.05 in February 1991. GDP: ZK22.495m ($1,800m) in 1988.

Growth of GDP: 0.9% per year 1970-82; -2% in 1988. GDP per capita: (1988) $290. Average inflation rate: 1970-82 was 8% per year. The inflation rate increased to an average of 80% in 1990. GDP by economic activity (1983): Agriculture 13.5% in 1990, mining 12.5%, and manufacturing 35%. Imports: $1,080m. Exports: $1,100m.

Religion: Protestant 31%, Roman Catholic 22%, Nominal 11%, Traditional 10%, African Independent Churches 8%, Islam 5% (estimate), Anglican 0.6%.

HISTORICAL BACKGROUND

Civilization in Zambia dates back many thousands of years. Settlement of the present people probably began about 1200 AD. With the exception of the Bushmen and Twa, the people are of Bantu origin, descendents of migrants from the Congo region.

Portuguese explored the eastern part of what is now Zambia in 1514. David Livingstone of Scotland explored the Zambezi basin in the late nineteenth century.

In 1889, Cecil Rhodes obtained treaties and concessions from chiefs in the area and a Royal Charter from Britain to establish government and trade. He also secured mineral concessions. By 1911, Northern Rhodesia had been formed, and was under the control of the British South Africa Company. In 1924, a legislative council that excluded Africans was established under British administration.

In 1953, against the wishes of most of the Africans in Northern Rhodesia, the Central African Federation was formed, uniting Northern and Southern Rhodesia and Nyasaland. Nationalist movements strongly opposed this federation and finally led to its dissolution in 1963. Independence was gained in 1964, and the country's name was changed to Zambia.

In 1972, Dr. Kenneth Kaunda moved away from a Westminster type of government to a one-party state. He introduced a new constitution embracing humanism as its guiding principle. The government has now committed itself to a multi-party democracy.

THE PEOPLE

With a growth rate of 3.6 percent each year, the projected population for the year 2000 is 11 million, placing a heavy burden on housing, health and educational facilities. Forty-nine percent of the people are in the 0-14 age group.

The people of Zambia are migrating from rural to urban areas. In 1960 only 23 percent of the population lived in towns and cities. Gradually, as mining began to draw rural dwellers to the urban copperbelt, the urbanization rate rose 7.4 percent annually. By 1989 about 54 percent of the population lived in towns. One-third of the population now lives along the copperbelt where seven of Zambia's ten towns are located.

Seventy-three ethnic groups speaking 80 identified languages live in Zambia. The seven major groups are:

- The *Bemba* people are the largest group and are of Zairian origin. Eighteen Bemba tribes make up 35 percent of the population. Bemba is spoken by most people in the copperbelt. Some 50 percent of the population understand Bemba.

- The *Tonga* people are in eight tribes and account for 17 percent of the population. They live in the south-central area of Zambia.

- The *Nyanja* people, with five tribes, account for 16 percent of the population. About 40 percent of the population speak and understand Nyanja.

- The *Lunda-Luvale* people, with six tribes in the northwest, make up 12.1 percent of the population.

- The *Barotse* group of 14 tribes, comprise 9.7 percent of the population. They are dominated by the Lozi tribe, and live in the plains of the Zambezi in the southwest part of Zambia.

- The *Mambwe*, living in the northeast, originated in Tanzania.

- The *Tukumbe* live in the eastern region of Zambia.

SOCIOECONOMIC CONDITIONS

Zambia's economy is based on copper, which accounts for 90 percent of its exports. After independence, the economy grew rapidly, but the decline in copper prices led to serious economic problems. The country's external debt has soared to about seven billion U.S dollars. Prospects for a stronger economy have improved since Zambia reached an agreement with the International Monetary Fund on a restructuring program. Debts have now been rescheduled as a result of these new initiatives and it is hoped that the economy will grow. With inflation running at 80 percent, however, wage increases do not match inflation increases. Lower income groups are particularly affected. There are calls for economic reforms.

Health

Government reports indicate that the overall health situation has deteriorated over the past five years. Services are limited by critical shortages of drugs and inefficient health systems. A primary health care system has been implemented but it is depends on poor transport systems and a restricted supply of drugs. This has resulted in a high infant mortality rate and an increase in other deaths. Malaria is rife and AIDS is placing a heavy burden on the over-loaded health service. Cholera is endemic in the north and is claiming the lives of many. A recent grant from Sweden may assist in improving health care over a three-year period.

Agriculture

Of the total land area, 5 percent is cultivated, a further 5 percent is arable and 40 percent has agricultural potential. Land tenure creates difficulties for those wanting to change to modern farming methods. There is a marked disparity between the 900 commercial farmers and subsistence farmers. Much of the subsistence farming sector is in the hands of women. The increase in maize productivity has been encouraging, but transporting the crop to markets presents difficulties.

Education

Although the official literacy rate is estimated to be 59 percent, UNESCO estimates the number of functionally literate adults has fallen to 24 percent. Illiteracy is high in rural areas. Records show that 80 percent of primary school age and 24 percent of high school age children are in school. The government sees education as a priority, and increasing emphasis is being placed on skills training. Night schools and correspondence schools are upgrading adult education. English is the language of instruction.

Socioeconomic disparities between rural and urban dwellers were inherited at independence, and this imbalance gave birth to Dr Kaunda's humanism ideology. A re-distribution of wealth, however, has not occurred under the current policies. About 10 percent of the population controls 46 percent of the national income. Education and health systems are still weighted in favor of urban dwellers.

Table 1: SOCIAL INDICATORS IN BRIEF

Total enrollment in education (1986)	1,605,949
% enrollment in primary education	90%
% enrollment in secondary education	9%
% enrollment in tertiary education	1%
Literacy rate	59%
Population per hospital and health care center bed	292
Population per physician (1981)	7,800
Population per nurse (1981)	1,600
Infant mortality rate (1987)	80 per 1,000
Population in 0-14 age group	49%
Life expectancy (1987)	53 years

STATUS OF CHRISTIANITY

Historical review

The history of missions in Zambia began with the arrival of David Livingstone in 1851. The purpose of his historic and extensive travels was to explore the interior of Africa, but at the end of his first journey traversing the continent from east to west, he wrote, "I view the end of the geographical feat as the beginning of the missionary enterprise." On his return to Scotland, he appealed for people to commit their lives to the missionary task. Frederick Arnot, a playmate of Livingstone's children, was the first Christian missionary to enter the part of Africa that would later become Zambia.

Initial missionary enterprise in Zambia was full of difficulties and discouragement. Arnot, a Plymouth Brethren missionary, arrived in Barotseland in 1882 and tried to work among the Lozi people. His attempts to establish a school were unsuccessful, and after eighteen months he moved west to Angola.

Basotho evangelists and Frances Coillard, a missionary from the Paris Missionary Society, established the first permanent missionary thrust into Northern Rhodesia. Other early entrants were sent by the London Missionary Society, the Primitive Methodist Church and the Dutch Reformed Church.

In 1886, Arnot returned from Angola and began to work with the Lunda people. Before the close of 1890, five Protestant mission stations had been established. Early Roman Catholic missions were the White Fathers and the Jesuits.

By 1910, the missionary advance was largely complete. In the east were Primitive Methodists, Brethren in Christ, Jesuits, Seventh Day Adventists and the Nyasa Industrial Mission. In the north, London Missionary Society, White Fathers and Livingstonia Mission (Free Church of Scotland) were established. The Dutch Reformed Church begun work in the south and the Paris Evangelical Mission in the west.

As an indirect means of spreading the gospel, missionaries opened schools, hospitals and clinics, but this did not result in rapid growth in church membership. In 1924, at a meeting of the Missionary Conference of Northern Rhodesia, it was established that, of the population of 1.5 million, no more than 18,000 had been baptized (1.2% of the population).

Disease took its toll on missionaries. The Paris Evangelical Missionary Society was particularly hard hit. By 1926, 22 adults and several children had lost their lives.

The church today

The Zambian constitution allows for "freedom of thought and religion, freedom to change his religion, or belief, and freedom to propagate his religion or belief in worship, teaching, practice and observance." Religious instruction is part of the school curriculum, but the syllabus includes religions other than Christianity, including humanism.

It is respectable to go to church in Zambia and the sense of belonging is important, but the church struggles to encourage commitment. Many mainline churches, especially in rural areas, have become syncretistic.

Gradually, as the church is reaching out to nominal Christians and to those who have never heard the gospel, churches are being renewed and, in most of the denominations, congregations are growing and spreading throughout the country. Facilities are being expanded to accommodate more people.

Student organizations on campuses and at colleges are making a tremendous impact, and many young people are committing their lives to Jesus Christ. They are being attracted to these growing churches, while older people tend to gravitate to churches where a more traditional and in some cases, a more syncretistic form of worship is practiced.

Possibly the greatest challenge to Christianity today is the desire of Muslims to win Zambia for Islam. A massive Islamic proselytization program is under way backed by money from the Arab nations. Muslims distribute food to needy people and pour money into mosques and educational facilities. Many Zambians living in the east and along the copperbelt have received financial aid from Muslims and accepted the Muslim faith.

UNREACHED PEOPLES

There is little evangelistic endeavor specifically geared to reach Muslims, or to counter their evangelistic zeal. There are about 30,000 to 50,000 Muslims, including an uncertain number of black Muslims. A number of Yao and Chichewa speaking Muslims live in the east along the Malawi border.

Communications in Zambia are poor, making it difficult to reach rural people. This is especially true of the Tongas in the Gwembe Valley, the Lozis in the west and others in the north and northwest.

Hindus in Zambia number approximately 10,000. The Evangelical Church in Zambia supports one couple who ministers to Hindus.

Baha'i groups meet in over 1,400 localities and gather more than 10,000 people. There is currently no Christian witness to people of Baha'i faith.

Jehovah's Witnesses are particularly active in Zambia and their publications are distributed in all the main Zambian languages. Their membership is estimated to be 67,000, with a further 381,000 adherents.

NATIONAL CHURCHES

Because of early missionary influence certain denominations developed in specific areas, but this localization is now breaking down.

Cooperation between missionary societies was evident early in the history of the country, and the first Missionary Conference of North-West Rhodesia was held in 1914. This led to a series of conferences held every three or four years until the General Missionary Conference of 1932 was established.

A number of councils currently promote cooperation among denominations and church groups:

• The Christian Council of Zambia (CCZ) has thirteen member churches, and acts as a coordinating body, particularly in the field of relief and development.

• The Episcopalian Conference of Zambia is a Catholic body operating on the same lines as EFZ and CCZ.

• The Evangelical Fellowship of Zambia (EFZ) is growing rapidly and now has 52 members, and is seeking to involve women in evangelism.

• The Pentecostal Fellowship of Zambia is in the process of being established.

Table 2: ESTIMATED RELIGIOUS AFFILIATION

Protestants [1]	31%
Roman Catholics	22%
Marginal Christians [2]	12%
Traditional religions	10%
African Independent [1]	8%
Muslims [3]	5%
Anglicans	0.6%

[1] Includes a percentage for the children of church members
[2] Figures given by the Jehovah's Witnesses and New Apostolic Church
[3] Estimated figure

Denominational membership is summarized in Table 3. Smaller church groups are not included.

Table 3: ESTIMATED CHURCH MEMBERSHIP [1]

Roman Catholic	1,627,000
United Church of Zambia	750,000
New Apostolic Church	434,510
Reformed Church in Zambia	133,000
Seventh Day Adventists	120,000
African Methodist Episcopal	82,000
Christian Brethren	75,000
Anglican	45,000
Evangelical Church in Zambia	31,600
Baptist Convention of Zambia	30,000
Pentecostal Assemblies of God	25,000
Church of God Zambia Region	20,000
Churches of Christ	17,000
Salvation Army	15,000
Baptist Union	15,000
Pentecostal Holiness Church	14,918
Apostolic Faith Mission in Zambia	14,000
Pilgrim Wesleyan Church	13,000
Brethren in Christ	12,000
Christian Fellowship of Zambia	10,500
Lutheran Church of Central Africa	10,000
Pilgrim Holiness Church	4,000
Presbyterian Church in Zambia	3,494

[1] *Includes adherents*

Roman Catholic Church

Portuguese priests made excursions into the area in the eighteenth century but did not attempt to establish a church.

The Jesuits tried to work in Zambia in 1879 and in 1882, but both missions failed. In 1905, the Jesuit Fathers (Society of Jesus) eventually began work in what is now the copperbelt. By 1923, they had established eight mission stations with 4,650 communicants and 88 schools.

The first Catholic mission to take root in the country was the White Fathers. They arrived at Mambwe in 1891 and began a ministry. In 1895, they founded a mission station at Kayambi. The work prospered, and one year later they had 500 boarders in their school. Their desire was to penetrate Bemba country and transform Bembaland into a Roman Catholic enclave. By emphasizing education and medical care, they made rapid advances.

The process of developing from mission to church was a gradual one. Initially, laity were given leadership positions in local congregations, and in 1920, a system of "elders" was introduced.

The hierarchy was established in 1959 and the Apostolic Nunciature was established in 1965, headed now by His Excellency the Most Reverend Eurenio Sbarbaro. He is responsible for the two Zambian archdioceses and is also the papal representative for Malawi.

Today, 219 churches have 1.6 million members. Nearly 600 priests minister to this large Catholic community. The Archdiocese of Lusaka has five dioceses under its control. They are in Chipata, Livingstone, Monze, Ndola and Solwezi. The Archdiocese of Kasama comprises the Mbala and Mansa Diocese.

The Roman Catholic Church is deeply involved in social action, operating 31 hospitals and clinics. In addition to ten institutions and children's homes, Catholics are also involved in community development project work and training.

From the start, African priests were required to undergo the same training as white priests, and on completion of this training, were given equal authority. By 1971, 16 percent of clergy or 62 priests were Zambian, and 380 priests were expatriates. Today, there are 450 priests, of whom 82 are Zambians (18%).

Training for the priesthood takes place at two major seminaries. Theological training is in Lusaka and philosophical training in Kabwe. A study center for Sisters is in Lusaka.

Anglican Church

Bishop Hine entered the country in 1910 and spent four years exploring the country on foot before selecting four sites to establish mission stations. Ministry to white settlers living in the towns was also developed and this has resulted in a strong urban work. The first three national priests were ordained in 1932. Clergy train at the United Church of Zambia College at Kitwe. The number of church members is about 45,000, but membership records are not kept to confirm this figure.

Protestant churches

UNITED CHURCH OF ZAMBIA

In 1925, Zambia experienced dramatic changes when rich copper deposits were discovered and copper mining began. Overnight, thousands of rural people were drawn to the copperbelt — an area with limited Christian presence.

While mission boards were deliberating as to whether to send workers, a spontaneous movement took place among the African miners. At Ndola, an autonomous African congregation developed with its own church government, paid evangelists, and extension works at Nchanga and Mufulira. They built their own church, naming it "Union Church of the Copperbelt."

In 1929, the Baptist missionary, the Reverend A.J. Cross wrote, "A self-supporting, self-governing native church has grown up and it is daily growing in strength and experience."

During the slump in the mining industry in 1931, Protestant missions joined the Union Church in supporting educational programs and welfare work in an effort known as the United Missions in the Copperbelt. The Union Church continued to grow rapidly, and in the years 1938-1940, it increased its membership by 60 percent.

In 1958 the London Mission Society and Church of Scotland Mission (previously merged) joined with the Union Church of the Copperbelt to form the Church of Central Africa in Rhodesia. In 1965, they united with the Methodist Church and the Church of Barotseland (Paris Evangelical Mission) to form the United Church of Zambia.

With an estimated membership of 750,000 in 648 churches cared for by 200 pastors, this church has become the largest Protestant church in Zambia and continues to grow rapidly.

REFORMED CHURCH IN ZAMBIA

An African evangelist from the Dutch Reformed mission base in Malawi travelled westward to preach the gospel in Ngoni country. His initiative resulted in a request from the chief to send teachers. Two evangelists were sent to investigate the need. Based on their favorable report, two Dutch Reformed missionaries, J.M. Hofmeyer and P.J. Smit, arrived in 1899 to establish the first mission station at Magwero. The work exanded, and by 1944, there were ten mission stations in the eastern part of Zambia. Preaching was accompanied by medical work, educational facilities, industrial and agricultural projects. Initially, the church was associated with the work in Malawi but in 1943, a separate synod of sixteen congregations was formed. In 1966, control was handed over to the national church.

The church was responsible for 88 primary schools and a secondary school at Katete that were handed over to the government in 1976. Hospitals at Nyanje and Kamoto remain under care of the church, but the clinics at the various mission stations were transferred to the government. Special schools caring for the blind and deaf are at Magwero.

The church has grown steadily. There were 50,000 members cared for by 58 ministers in 1980. Today the church has about 133,000 members and affiliates.

Ministers are trained at Justo Mwale Theological College in Lusaka. Applicants need university-level schooling to register.

EVANGELICAL CHURCH IN ZAMBIA

Africa Evangelical Fellowship (then South Africa General Mission) was started by Albert Bailey in 1910, when he established a ministry among the Kaonde people in the North-Western province. The work grew rapidly to reach the Western province, and more recently the copperbelt towns. The 677 churches and extension ministries are now the responsibility of the Evangelical Church in Zambia, the church that grew out of the work of the mission. Expatriate missionaries are called "fellowship workers."

The Evangelical Church is involved in literature ministry, and operates six bookshops and a wholesale division. Christian Broadcasting Fellowship produces programs for radio and television. Two hospitals and a secondary school are under their care.

The Theological College of Central Africa at Ndola, started by the Evangelical Church, has now been handed over to the Evangelical Fellowship of Zambia. The church has two Bible schools and a number of Theological Education by Extension (TEE) courses operating across the country.

The Evangelical Church is continuing to grow rapidly and has 22,600 members and a further 9,000 new believers.

CHRISTIAN BRETHREN

Fred Arnot was the first missionary to enter Zambia. His first efforts to establish a work in Barotseland were unsuccessful and he moved westward. After successfully starting a ministry in Zaire, he re-entered Zambia in 1897. Medical work was established and the church grew rapidly. By 1923, twelve mission stations had been established. Today, the Christian Brethren church has an estimated 75,000 members.

BAPTIST CHURCH

The first Baptists in Zambia were missionaries of the South African Baptist Missionary Society who arrived in 1905. The Reverend A. J. Cross of the Kafulafuta Mission became involved in a spontaneous movement among the miners, which was later to result in the Union Church of the Copperbelt.

In 1976, the Zambian Baptist Union was formed bringing together the Zambian Baptist Association (formerly the Baptist Union of Central Africa), the Northern Baptist Association (a union of Australian Baptists and the Lambaland work) and the Mpongwe Baptist Association (Swedish).

The Baptist Union has a hospital at Mpongwe, and Bible school at Fiwale Hill. Church members number 15,000.

The Southern Baptist Foreign Mission Board began work in Zambia in the early sixties, concentrating efforts along the copperbelt and Lusaka area. Missionaries opened a publishing center in Lusaka that included a recording studio for the production of broadcast tapes. The Baptist Theological Seminary of Zambia is in Lusaka. The Baptist Convention of Zambia, the church that developed from the work of the mission, has grown rapidly and continues to grow numerically and spread to other parts of the country. Membership is estimated to be 30,000.

Seventh Day Adventists entered the country in 1905. They have worked mainly among the Bemba and Tonga people. Church members number 120,000. The increase in church growth is currently 20 percent a year. Ministries include two hospitals.

New charismatic churches are growing rapidly and comprise many small indepedendent groups. These include:

- Christian Fellowship of Zambia
- Deeper Christian Life Ministry Fire Baptised Church
- New Life Ministries
- Open Door Christian Centres.
- Pentecostal Believers Church
- Victory Bible Church

The New Apostolic Church is one of the largest church groups in the country, with 434,500 members operating in 41 districts. Its theology is of the Catholic Apostolic tradition, and is considered to be sectarian. The church's leaders have no formal training. It is particularly strong in the southwestern region among the Lozi and Tonga people.

Indigenous churches

There are about seventy indigenous churches in Zambia. Some of these have been introduced from neighboring states such as South Africa, Malawi, Zaire and Zimbabwe, while others are breakaways from established churches and missions like the Catholic, Reformed, Brethren and United churches. These movements combine Africa's religious and cultural heritage with Christian beliefs. Indigenous churches seldom become involved in institutional work or social action.

The Reverend Coillard, a French pioneer missionary, was the first to experience an indigenous attempt to break away from his mission, when a Basotho evangelist introduced "Ethiopian" teaching and tried to start a new work. This attempt was short-lived, but others have prospered since then.

The most notable of these has been the Lumpa Church. Alice Lenshina Mulenga, the prophetess, claimed to have been raised from the dead and to have had a vision of receiving two books from heaven. In 1956 up to 1,000 people a week were making a pilgrimage to visit her. Her teaching embraced Christian principles and was anti-witchcraft. By 1958, the Lumpa Church was well established. After independence, the government became involved in military clashes with Lumpa Church followers — clashes that eventually cost 700 lives. The church was banned and Alice Lenshina imprisoned. She was released from detention in 1975 and died in 1978.

Indigenous churches with large followings include:

- Africa Gospel Church
- Africa National Church
- Apostles in Zion Church
- Apostolic Faith (Holy Gospel) Church
- Catholic Church of the Sacred Heart
- Central Africa Church
- Gospel Seventh-Day Church of Zambia
- Holy Spirit Zion Church
- Independent Watchtower Church
- Watchman Healing Mission

FOREIGN MISSIONARIES

Approximately 600 Protestant expatriate missionaries work in Zambia, with most involved in the institutional and development work under national churches. Missionaries also train leaders. Societies working in Zambia include:

- Africa Evangelical Fellowship
- Brethren Assemblies
- Christian Missions in Many Lands
- Church of the Nazarene
- Church of Scotland
  Board of World Missions
- Dutch Reformed Church
- Lutheran World Federation
- Mennonite Central Committee
- Pentecostal Assemblies of God
- Salvation Army
- Seventh Day Adventists
  General Conference
- Southern Baptist Convention
  Foreign Missions
- United Church of Canada
- United Society for the
  Propagation of the Gospel
- Wesleyan Church World Mission

CHRISTIAN ACTIVITIES

Evangelism

Many Zambians are finding new faith in Christ. Student or ganizations have been at the forefront of this missionary zeal. Scripture Union works among secondary school students and in primary schools. Zambian Fellowship of Evangelical Students evangelizes on campuses and in colleges. Nurses Christian Fellowship is having an impact on hospital staff. The ripple effect of these organizations is felt in many churches.

The majority of denominations have their own evangelism programs that are bringing about rapid church growth.

Every Home for Christ has reached a million homes with Christian literature since 1981. Home visits are followed up with correspondence courses available in eight languages.

Campaigns conducted by Christ for All Nations have been conducted in four centers.

Africa Enterprise has also been involved in mass campaigns.

Institute for Church Growth is active in leadership training.

Broadcasting

In 1984 there were an estimated one million radios and 240,000 television sets in Zambia.

Multimedia operates religious television and radio programs on the national network. It is managed jointly by the Zambian Episcopal Conference and the Zambia Christian Council, presenting two hours of television and fifteen hours of radio each week.

Evangelical Church of Zambia produces programs for Zambia Broadcasting Services and Trans World Radio. A weekly children's program is prepared for television. They also produce cassettes with Bible studies, messages and music in Zambian languages.

The Baptist Convention of Zambia has a recording studio in Lusaka, providing cassettes in ethnic languages.

Trans World Radio transmits programs in English from its station in Swaziland.

Literature

"The neglect and emptiness of appropriate literature indicates that we are committing intellectual and moral suicide," stated Dr. Kenneth Kaunda in a speech on the value of literature. This is true of Christian as well as secular literature. Although sixteen Christian bookshops in Zambia serve most of the towns, the majority of these shops have empty shelves. Furthermore, most bookshops are along the railway line and rural areas are neglected. The Bible Society has established a depot on the copperbelt and reports good sales.

There is little Christian literature available to meet the needs of college and university graduates. Some dialects have no Christian literature at all.

Little is published within Zambian, and lack of foreign exchange makes importing of books difficult. Most published materials are translations from other countries. Only about one percent are written by nationals, with the rest written by missionaries. Christian publishers include:

- Africa Christian Books
- Baptist Publishing House
- Bible Society of Zambia
- Copperbelt Christian Publications
- Daystar Publications
- Multimedia Zambia
- Scripture Union
- Seventh Day Adventists
- UCZ Publications

Scripture distribution

Early missionaries emphasized the translation of the Scriptures into local languages, and by 1928, Scriptures were available in fifteen languages.

The full Bible is available in Bemba, Tonga, Nyanja, Namwanga, Chokwe, Kunda, Mambwe, Lunda, Kaonde, Silozi, Luchazi, Chichewa, Tumbuku and English.

A new translation of the Tonga Bible is in process. The new Silozi translation was published in 1986.

Despite the high cost of living, the sale of Bibles and Scripture portions exceeded expectations. The Bible Society distributed 206,527 Bibles, 55,234 New Testaments and more than 500,000 portions of Scripture during 1987.

Christian education

There are many seminaries and Bible colleges in Zambia, the majority of which are denominational.

The Theological College of Central Africa, belonging to the Evangelical Fellowship of Zambia, is the only college in Zambia that offers degrees. It has been granted accreditation by ACTEA.

The Evangelical Church has Bible institutes at Chizela and Luampa Mission.

The Baptist Union of Zambia has a Bible college at Fiwale, near Ndola.

The Baptist Theological Seminary of Zambia (Baptist Convention of Zambia) is in Lusaka. They are working toward accreditation.

Roman Catholics train priests at St Dominic's Major Seminary and St Augustine's Major Seminary. Sisters in formation are trained at the Kalundu Study Centre in Lusaka.

The United Church of Zambia Theological College at Kitwe serves the Anglican church.

The Pentecostal Holiness Church trains Christian workers at Emmanuel Bible Institute at Kitwe.

Justo Mwale Theological College trains post secondary students for the Reformed Church of Zambia ministry. They are working toward offering degrees.

Other colleges include:

- Christian Institute of Leadership Training (Church of Christ)
- Foundation Bible School (Church of God)
- Kaniki Bible College (Apostolic Church in Zion)
- Lutheran Bible Institute and Seminary
- Nazarene Bible School
- Pentecostal Assemblies of God Bible College
- Pilgrim Wesleyan Seminary
- Salvation Army Training College
- Sikalongo Bible Institute (Brethren in Christ)
- Victory Bible Institute

In addition, a number of these colleges offer Theological Education by Extension and correspondence courses.

Theological Education by Extension in Zambia (TEEZ) is at Mindola. It is a joint project of several churches to train church leaders in their various ministries. Currently, 2,000 people are involved in their training courses across Zambia.

World Outreach in Lusaka reports that 15,000 students are enrolled in their correspondence courses.

Social concerns

Missionary participation in health care and education dates back to the beginning of Christian witness. The first medical doctors arrived in 1887, and by 1910 five missionary societies had doctors in the field.

Today, 30 of 83 hospitals in Zambia are mission hospitals and are government subsidized. Clinics are now operated by the Ministry of Health.

Churches involved in medical work include:

- Anglican church

- Baptist Union of Zambia
- Brethren in Christ
- Evangelical Church of Zambia
- Pentecostal Holiness Church
- Reformed Church of Zambia
- Roman Catholics
- Seventh Day Adventists
- United Church of Zambia

Education in Zambia was started by missionary societies. The British colonial government began providing subsidies in 1924 and mission influence in education gradually decreased. Today, the government is totally responsible for education.

SPECIAL NEEDS IN ZAMBIA

- Pastors who have been in the ministry for a number of years need refresher courses. Upgrading academic qualifications followed by further theological training would give them the confidence needed to relate to younger and better-educated members of their congregations. Most Zambians consider that formal training is better than "on-the-job" training since formal training will be more likely to produce confident leaders who can initiate programs.

- Churches should accept greater responsibility for supporting pastors and Christian workers. Current levels of remuneration present difficulties in attracting younger people to the ministry.

- To help the Zambian church in its desire to be self-sufficient, mission agencies could consider diverting their funds to train Zambian leaders rather than send expatriate workers.

- Zambian Christians want training in publishing, printing and distribution.

- Women are in the majority in most of the mainline churches. Need-based ministries to reach men are required.

- New ways of reaching traditionalists should be explored. Unreached people need to be identified and contextualized churches planted.

- The rapid increase in the incidence of AIDS challenges the church to be relevant to young adults.

BIBLIOGRAPHY

ACTEA *Directory of Theological Schools in Africa*, 1985.

Africa Research Bulletin, Africa Research Ltd.

Africa South of the Sahara 1989, Europa Publications.

Barrett, David, *World Christian Encyclopaedia*, Oxford University Press.

Bolink, Peter, *Towards Church Union in Zambia: A Study of Missionary Co-operation and Church Union in Central Africa*, T. Wever, 1967.

Catholic Directory 1987/88, S.A. Catholic Bishop's Conference.

Central Statistical Office Lusaka, Monthly Digest of Statistics, May/August 1986.

Economist Intelligence Unit, *Zambia Country Profile, 1990/91*.

Economist Intelligence Unit, *Zambia Country Report, January 1991*.

Encyclopaedia of the Third World, Mansell.

Fair T.J.D., *Zambia: The Search for Rural/Urban Balance*, Africa Institute.

Munguya, Arnot, *A General Survey of Christian Literature Work in Zambia*, Project Literature for South Africa, Potchefstroom University for Christian Higher Education.

Randall, Max Ward, "Profile for Victory," *New Profiles for Missions in Zambia*, William Carey, 1970 .

Rotberg, Robert I., *Christian Missionaries and the Creation of Northern Rhodesia 1880-1924*, Princeton University, 1965.

Smith, Edwin, *The Way of the White Fields in Rhodesia 1886-1924*, World Dominion Press, 1928.

Taylor, John V. and Lehmann, Dorothea, *Christians of the Copperbelt*, SCM Press.

Verstraelen-Gilhuis, Gerdien, *From Dutch Mission Church to Reformed Church in Zambia*, T. Wever, 1982.

Woodhall, Chester, *Churches and Development Directory For Zambia*, Mindolo Ecumenical Foundation.

World Vision International Zambia Office, *Country Strategy 1986-1990*.

REPUBLIC OF ZIMBABWE

Co-edited by Phineas Dube

Profile

Natural features: Land area of 390,580 km^2 (150,803 sq miles). This landlocked country shares borders with South Africa, Botswana, Zambia and Mozambique. The terrain is rolling plateau with three regions: Highveld, with peaks of up to 2,595 meters (8,500 feet) in the east; the Middleveld; and the Lowveld, generally below 1,000 meters (3,280 feet) in altitude.

Climate: Most of the country has a temperate climate with average temperatures ranging from 13-30°C (56-83°F). Average annual rainfall ranges from 1,400 mm a year (55 inches) in the Highveld to 800 mm a year (31inches) in the Lowveld.

Population: 9.12 million (1989 estimate). Annual growth rate: 3.5%. Population density: 23 per km^2 (60 per square mile) (1985 est). Population in 0-14 age group: 48% (1982).

Ethnic groups: Two main groups: Shona and Ndebele with ethnic ratio of 4:l. The Shona people are comprised of several groups, including the Karanga (40% of total population), Zezeru, Manyika, Korekore and Ndau. Whites: 90,000.

Language and literacy: English is the official language, but Shona and Ndebele are widely used. Literacy rate: 60%.

Urbanization: 30%. Urban Growth Rate: 6.3% per year. Capital: Harare (900,000). Other cities include Bulawayo (495,000); Chitungwiza (173,000); Gweru (79,000); and Mutare (75,000).

Government: Republic with executive authority vested in the President, Mr. Robert Mugabe. Parliament consists of a Senate and House of Assembly. There are eight provinces. Government is centralized.

Economy: Currency: 100 cents = 1 Zimbabwe dollar. Z$2.45 = US$1 (Average 1990); Z$2.9 (April 1991) = US$1. GDP (1990): Z$13,029; GDP per capita (1990): Z$1,428. Inflation rate (1989): 15%. Exports (1990): Z$1,580m; Imports: Z$1,500m; Agriculture as % of GDP (1990): 12.7%; Manufacturing: 26.5%; Mining: 7.1%. Growth rate (1982- 87): 1%; (1990) 1.9%.

Religion: Traditional 43%; Protestant 31%; African Independent churches 12%; Roman Catholic 8%; Anglican 3%; Non-Christian 2%; Marginal Christian 1%.

HISTORICAL BACKGROUND

The ruins of Great Zimbabwe date back to approximately the twelth century, giving indication of a well organized and complex early settlement. In a later era, the Ndebele King Lobengula ruled until 1893, when Cecil Rhodes obtained a Royal charter to exploit mineral rights and overthrew the king.

The British South Africa Company administered Southern Rhodesia, as it was then called, until it was annexed by Britain in 1923. In 1953, Southern Rhodesia joined with Northern Rhodesia and Nyasaland briefly to form the Central African Federation.

Resistance to the policies of the colonial government grew into a bitter liberation war lasting until independence in 1980. President Robert Mugabe is a dedicated Marxist and the governing ZANU (Zimbabwe African National Union) party adopted a Marxist-Leninist ideology. Party policy as stated at its 1984 congress had the following two objectives:

· The restructuring and reconstruction of the national economy so as to ensure the victory of socialism over capitalism; and

· The establishment of a socialist state based on Marxist-Leninist principles.

Despite these clearly articulated goals, pragmatism has prevailed and the government has not taken any significant steps towards scientific socialism.

In December 1989, a new political party brought together ZANU and Joshua Nkomo's party to form ZANU-PF. Elections in 1990 resulted in a sweeping victory for Mugabe who retains his position as president. Public resistance to the proposed one-party state has resulted in the idea being shelved. A state of emergency, operative since 1965, was lifted in July 1990.

SOCIOECONOMIC CONDITIONS

Zimbabwe has the status of being one of Africa's most economically advanced nations, inheriting a well developed and diversified economy at independence. Unfortunately, high unemployment, rising inflation, high cost of debt servicing, drastic cuts in import allocations, and involvement in the Mozambican war have slowed economic growth. Talks with the World Bank have taken place, and a measure of liberalization is occurring.

The country is rich in minerals. Agriculture, however, is the backbone of the economy, with tobacco as the main crop.

Zimbabwe aims to be self-sufficient in food and it already provides its own maize needs. The 1988 harvest was a record crop.

About 4,400 white commercial farmers own 40 percent of the land. Proposed changes to the Land Act is causing a constitutional crisis and could affect economic output.

Education and labor

The government recognizes primary education as a right of every Zimbabwean, and is committed to providing secondary education to all primary school graduates. The result has been massive increases in enrollment in schools since 1979. In primary schools, the enrollment increase was 170 percent, while in secondary schools the increase was more than 700 percent. No less then 12 percent of the GDP is spent on education.

This tremendous achievement, however, has also presented a problem. Few opportunities are available in the labor market. Of the 300,000 graduates each year, only about 8,000 find jobs in the formal sector. This falls short of optimistic forecasts predicting 30,000 new jobs each year. Only 12 percent of the population is currently employed in the formal sector, compared with 17 percent in 1982. Since the majority of graduates will have a secondary education, it is unlikely that they will be satisfied to work in communal lands as peasant farmers or in the urban informal sector. This situation could have serious implications for the stability of the country.

Health and welfare

Zimbabwe's health strategy is based on a primary health-care system with community involvement. Since 1980, more than 4,000 village health workers have been trained. The long-term goal is to have one health worker for every 500 people. The Ministry of Health is the largest provider of health services. Missions and churches, who are 100 percent grant-aided, local authorities, industry and private practitioners also contribute to health care. The AIDS epidemic has been given official recognition. It is estimated that 5 percent of the population is carrying the virus.

Table 1: SOCIAL INDICATORS IN BRIEF

Total enrollment in the education system	2,730,000
% enrollment in primary schools	81%
% enrollment in secondary schools	17.6%
% enrollment in tertiary education	1.2%
Pupil/teacher ratio	36:1
Literacy rate	60%
No. of hospitals, clinics and health posts	1,202

Population per hospital bed	624
Population per doctor (1985)	6,720
Population per nurse (1985)	570
Infant mortality rate (per 1000 live births)	72
Life expectancy at birth	57 years

STATUS OF CHRISTIANITY

Historical review

The first missionary to enter this area was a Portuguese Jesuit, Father Gonzalo da Silveira. He landed off the coast of Mozambique and made his way inland to meet Chief Monomatapa, arriving in 1560. He baptized 300 people within a month of his arrival. Eventually, the chief turned against him and he was murdered, becoming the first Christian martyr in Southern Africa. A century later, the Dominicans attempted to establish another work that was soon aborted.

Robert Moffat of the London Missionary Society, who arrived with his party in 1859, established the first lasting work. The Society secured land in the Inyati valley, but work among the warlike Ndebeles was difficult and not very successful. Before much time had passed, seven of the party of ten had died.

By the turn of the century, other missions and churches had established work in Zimbabwe. These included Roman Catholic Jesuits who arrived again in 1879, more than three centuries after their first attempt. Other groups with ministries at the turn of the century were: the Anglican church, the Dutch Reformed Church, (now the Reformed Church of Zimbabwe), the Methodist church (UK), the Salvation Army, the American Board Mission, the Seventh Day Adventist church, the South Africa General Mission (now the Africa Evangelical Fellowship), the Methodist church (USA), the Brethren in Christ Church, the Church of Christ, the Presbyterian church, and the Berlin Mission.

The church today

During the war, the church was severely affected. Churches and institutions were burned and the people scattered. Many whose faith had been nominal turned away from Christianity.

The years following independence have been years of reconstruction as the church tries to find its place within the framework of a government with socialist ideals. The constitution guarantees freedom of religion and the government has thus far not placed any restriction on the church. With independence came the search for national identity and attempts to blend Christianity with Zimbabwe culture. The country's former president, the Rev. Canaan Banana, stated: "Theology and the church must accommodate African experience and traditional religion."

The Shona people believe in a religion that provides a source of strength against evils that beset their path. Traditionally, the Shona have believed in higher powers, and perform religious functions associated with that belief.

The Shona social system is based on clans. Clan heads are important. While alive, the head of the clan is the representative of the ancestors. When dead, ancestors become the guardians of the clan. There is a close link between the living and the dead; each becomes dependent on the other for well-being. Fundamental, then, is the belief that the life spirit does not die. For a Shona Christian to make a break with traditional religion, however, is a major event because it involves the interruption of family forefather veneration. The issue of ancestral veneration is primary in the Zimbabwean church.

Four ancestral spirits are venerated on a national scale, the most prominent of which is Mbuya Nehanda. At independence, this spirit was publicly lauded for her success in the liberation war. Songs were written about her and recordings made and widely circulated.

Despite this, many in Zimbabwe, and especially young people, are returning to the churches. Charismatic churches are growing rapidly.

UNREACHED PEOPLES

As we see from the examples given above, a deep understanding of Shona culture is essential for those who seek to win Shona to the Lord.

The people of the Zambezi Valley are isolated and need church-planting ministries. These groups include the Tonga, Korekore (Shona sub-group), and San (Bushmen) people. Shangaans in the Chiredzi area are linguistically isolated.

About 6,500 Hindus of Indian origin have temples in Harare, Bulawayo, Mutare and Gweru.

The Muslim community includes Indian Muslims, black Muslims (mainly Yao, originally from Malawi), and Zimbabwean converts. Their affiliation is estimated to be 160,000. Muslims are aggressive in their outreach and are building mosques across the country.

About 27,000 people affiliated with the Baha'i religion meet at 194 localities.

Many of the 175,000 Mozambican refugees in Zimbabwe are from areas that are totally unreached by Christians, and have the opportunity to hear the gospel for the first time.

Educated urban elite who no longer fit into village life have shifted ideologically to the West or East. Widespread unemployment has brought disillusionment, a lack of direction, dualism, and a vacuum in many lives.

NATIONAL CHURCHES

Attempts to unify churches began early in Zimbabwe. The majority of churches and missionary societies joined the Southern Rhodesian Missionary Conference, which was formed in 1903. The Southern Rhodesian African Missionary Conference started in 1954. At independence, there were three bodies in the ecumenical scene: the Christian Conference of Rhodesia, now disbanded; the Christian Council of Rhodesia, now the Zimbabwe Christian Council; and the Evangelical Fellowship of Rhodesia. Today, unifying bodies include:

• *Zimbabwe Christian Council*, representing 28 denominations and organizations. Relief and development, one of their major ministries, is administered through Christian Care;

• *Evangelical Fellowship of Zimbabwe*, coordinating more than 40 churches and organizations;

• *Pentecostal Fellowship of Zimbabwe*, bringing together ten denominations;

• *Fambidzano* (African Independent Church Conference), an association of a number of the independent churches; and

• *Ministers' Fraternals*, drawing ministers from a number of denominations together.

The churches in Zimbabwe have joined forces in a DAWN (Discipling a Whole Nation) program to identify unevangelized areas and train church leaders to reach out in a church-planting ministry.

Table 2: ESTIMATED RELIGIOUS AFFILIATION

Traditional	43%
Protestant	31%
African Independent	12%
Roman Catholic	8%
Anglican	3%
Non Christian	2%
Marginal Christian	1%

Table 3: ESTIMATED MEMBERSHIP
FOR DENOMINATIONS LARGER THAN 2,000

Roman Catholic Church	674,461
Zimbabwe Assemblies of God	500,000
Church of the Province (Anglican)	229,000
Seventh Day Adventist church	136,631
Methodist Church in Zimbabwe (community)	100,754
United Methodist Church	60,000
Salvation Army	53,320
Reformed church	50,000
Apostolic Faith Mission	47,129
Evangelical Lutheran Church in Zimbabwe	44,000
African Methodist Episcopal Church	32,000
Evangelical Church of Zimbabwe	20,252
Church of Christ	14,000
Church of Christ (USA)	13,000
Baptist Convention of Zimbabwe	11,000
CCAP	7,564
Pentecostal Assemblies of Zimbabwe	7,000
Church of God Prophecy	6,759
Church of God World Missions (Full Gospel)	6,484
Assemblies of God USA	6,000
United Congregational Church	5,000
Presbyterian Church of Southern Africa	4,759
Brethren in Christ Church	4,500
Brethren Assemblies	4,000
United Apostolic Faith Church	3,000
Glad Tidings Fellowship	3,000
Baptist Union of Zimbabwe	2,500
The Evangelical Church	2,240
Nederduitse Hervormde Herk	2,162
Church of the Nazarene	2,137
Free Methodist Church	2,054
Alliance Church	2,000

Roman Catholic Church

The annals of the Catholic church are interwoven with the history of Zimbabwe since 1560, when Father Gonzalo da Silveira gave his life for his faith. Two further attempts were made to establish Catholicism, but in 1759, all missionary work ceased.

In 1879, Jesuits made a third attempt to establish work in Matabeleland, but after three years they had lost ten men without gaining one convert. Following years of discouragement, they decided to relocate their work and head north where a mission was established outside Salisbury (now Harare). The number of new locations then steadily increased. At each central mission, a church was built and a farm established. The Dominican Sisters developed elementary schools and health work.

Conflict between the Catholic church and the colonial government developed between 1959 and 1979, when the church identified itself with the struggle for liberation. The colonial government felt that the church was subversive, and deported several priests and nuns.

Since independence, the church has returned to identify itself with the country in the development of its people, and the church has grown rapidly. Today nearly 400 priests serve at 150 churches and missions, with many other outstations. The Catholic population is now estimated to be 674,000 in six dioceses.

The Catholic church runs 123 schools, mostly in rural areas. Their medical work is extensive and 28 Catholic hospitals include specialized tuberculosis sanatoriums, nurses training schools, and outlying clinics.

The majority of the clergy are expatriate workers, but indigenization is a goal of the church. There are three minor seminaries and a theological seminary at Gweru. Nearly 80 convents are scattered across the country. In 1980, Zimbabwe was established as an Apostolic Nunciature.

Anglican church

Bishop Knight Bruce of Bloemfontein in South Africa visited Mashonaland in 1888, and was challenged with the need to reach the Shona people. He made friends with a number of chiefs and was granted land. Bruce brought catechists in 1891, and after much difficulty, they reached the Mutare area. He and his assistant Bernard Mizeki visited neighboring chiefs who agreed to have teachers in their villages. By 1900, Anglican influence had spread to a number of other areas. Schools and medical centers were opened.

The years of the liberation war were difficult for the Anglican church. Many churches, schools, hospitals and clinics were destroyed during the war years. Furthermore, the church was seen as supporting the colonial government, which has presented difficulties after independence.

Today, the task of reconstruction of buildings is under way, and the church is growing. Ministry to youth has brought many to Christ. Formation of house churches has strengthened worship and commitment. Workshops have begun to train clergy to initiate lay training in their own areas.

Four dioceses minister to the spiritual and social needs of the people. The church plays an important role in the development process of the nation. Since membership records are not kept in this denomination, the figure of 229,000 members is an estimate.

Protestant churches

UNITED CONGREGATIONAL CHURCH OF SOUTHERN AFRICA

The work of the London Missionary Society in Zimbabwe was the vision of Robert Moffat, who first visited the area in 1829. Thirty years later, he led a party of missionaries to Matabeleland where land was given to them at Inyati. The mission planted was the first Protestant witness in the country. A further site was secured at Hopefontein. Nearly another 30 years elapsed before they saw their first convert to Christianity.

As the mission became established and further mission stations were opened, an emphasis on educational work developed. By 1903, 23 schools were operating. Churches grew slowly, and by 1937, the church had only 1,500 members. In 1967, the London Missionary Society, together with the American Board Mission, united to form the Zimbabwe Synod of the United Congregational Church of Southern Africa. Today, it has 5,000 members.

REFORMED CHURCH IN ZIMBABWE

African church members across the border in South Africa caught the vision for evangelism in Zimbabwe, and their efforts brought Shona people for instruction and baptism to the Reformed church in Zoutpansberg, South Africa. In 1891, the Dutch Reformed Mission Church was formally able to enter the country. Seven African evangelists and one expatriate missionary arrived at an area a few kilometers from the Great Zimbabwe ruins, where the chief gave them permission to establish a mission. They named the mission "Morgenster," and it became the first of a number of mission stations across the eastern part of the country.

Although the primary task of the mission was evangelism, it soon became involved in education and medicine. Only three years after the arrival of the first missionaries, a doctor joined them. Caring for the needs of the community has continued to play an important role in the work of this denomination. They established schools at all their stations and outstations, and also started teacher training colleges. Today, the church has homes for girls, a school for the blind, and a school for the deaf. It offers industrial and agricultural training, and produces literature.

In 1918, the Council of Congregations gave the churches jurisdiction over their congregations. In 1952, an autonomous church was formed, now called the Reformed Church of Zimbabwe. All missionaries became members of the local church.

The training of ministers started in 1925, prior to which teachers and evangelists were trained together. Murray Theological College at Morgenster now stands as a memorial to those early efforts. Current membership of the Reformed church is 50,000.

SALVATION ARMY

In 1891, the Salvation Army began working in Harare, where the organization's headquarters are located today. The Salvation Army grew rapidly, expanding into all provinces with its emphasis on social services. Today the Salvation Army ministers to more than 53,000 people at 512 corps and preaching points.

SEVENTH DAY ADVENTIST CHURCH

The Seventh Day Adventist church began work in 1895. The church has grown at a rate of 20 percent each year, and in 1989, had 136,631 members. Work has centered around the Bulawayo area with extensive education and agricultural programs. Dental clinics operate at Bulawayo and Mutare. A theological training institute offers university-level courses.

THE METHODIST CHURCH IN ZIMBABWE

The Methodist Church in Zimbabwe began ministry in 1891. Full and on-trial members total 64,000, but the Methodist community is estimated to total 100,754. Assisted by 4807 local preachers, 52 clergy and 30 evangelists minister in the country for a ratio of 1259 people per full-time minister.

Ministers are trained at the United Theological College, where 26 students are currently enrolled in a four-year course. The Methodist church has eight secondary schools. Some 60 children are cared for at the Matthew Rusike Children's Home.

THE UNITED METHODIST CHURCH

The United Methodist Church was an early entrant into Zimbabwe. American missionaries arrived in 1897 to work in the Mutare area. With a strong emphasis on social work, they developed community projects and established schools and hospitals. By 1927, 10,000 members were reported.

The church suffered heavy losses during the war, and membership declined dramatically. The post-war development programs, aimed at community development, leadership development and church reconstruction, have resulted in rapid growth. Today, church membership is estimated to be 60,000.

ZIMBABWE ASSEMBLIES OF GOD AFRICA

Zimbabwe Assemblies of God Africa, established in 1960, is an indigenous church movement that is growing rapidly. Today, about 500,000 people belong. Growth can be attributed to involvement in house churches and an evangelistic outreach aimed for youth called "Forward in Faith." A Bible school in Harare trains 120 students.

African independent churches

The first indigenous church began in 1906, but it was not until the 1920s that African independent churches became significant. Current statistics on the independent churches are not available, but it is estimated that members in these religious groups number half a million. Some of these churches originated in neighboring countries, while others are breakaways from missions and churches in Zimbabwe.

Zimbabwe has about 120 of these church groups. They generally fall into two categories: Zionists, of the Pentecostal and prophetic tradition, and the Ethiopian groups, which tend to follow the teachings of the mainline churches. Several of these groups incorporate aspects of traditional worship. Some of the larger groups include:

- African Apostolic Church of Johane Maranke
- African Congregational Church
- African Orthodox Church
- Apostolic Faith Church
- First Ethiopian Church
- Mai Chaza Church
- Masowe Church
- Soldiers of God
- Zion Apostolic Church
- Zion Christian Church

FOREIGN MISSIONARIES

Despite discouragement, early missionaries made a valuable contribution to the development of Zimbabwe. Not only did they establish churches and translate Scriptures, but they also established medical care, agricultural projects and schools. Education came to be the major means of growth in the churches.

The war of independence brought many changes. Missionary activity was constrained and many rural churches were forced to close. Many expatriate missionaries left the country at that time, while others moved into towns to establish urban ministries. The war also forced the Christian church to assess its relationship with the government. One of the early dissenters was Bishop Ralph Dodge of the United Methodist Church, who was deported in 1964 for his outspoken criticism of colonial government policies.

Since independence, a few new missionary societies have been allowed to enter the country. The government has given preference to those who contribute to the development of the country.

Work permits are becoming more difficult to obtain and the government expects missions and para-church organizations to train nationals to take over the work of expatriates. While there is still a need for highly skilled missionaries to assist in training and other specialized areas, the national church is taking the lead in reaching the nation for Christ.

CHRISTIAN ACTIVITIES

Evangelism

Social upheaval has caused the nation to turn to God, and people are becoming more open to the gospel. Whites have felt insecure, for example, and more are turning to Christianity as a result. In response, Christians are involved in a variety of evangelistic activities.

Large crusades have been held in urban areas by groups such as Christ for all Nations and Africa Enterprise. Many persons indicated their willingness to accept Christ, but these decisions do not always result in wholehearted commitment.

Africa Enterprise works in rural areas and refugee camps through a ministry called Operation Foxfire.

Life Ministry's *Jesus* film has been translated into Shona, Ndebele and Tonga. Pastors use it to establish new congregations. Life Ministry is training pastors in follow-up. This organization is also reaching out to professional men and politicians through its ministry to executives.

Scripture Union and its college counterpart FOCUS are reaching young people in schools and on college campuses, reporting that many students are turning to Christ.

Evangelism Explosion trains clergy and laity in evangelism. Gospel Recordings has material available in English, Ndebele, Kalanga and five Shona dialects.

Broadcasting

The Christian Broadcasting Association was formed to be a liason with the Zimbabwe Broadcasting Corporation on matters pertaining to religious services. Its members represent most of the large denominations.

Three denominations have studios in Zimbabwe: the Baptist Mission in Zimbabwe, the Evangelical Church, and the Reformed

Church in Zimbabwe. These three organizations and Trans World Radio, which operates from its radio station in Swaziland, prepare programs for transmission over the national service.

Gospel Recordings has recordings in the following languages: English, Kalanga, Lilima, Ndebele, Sili, Tsonga and Shona dialects of Chimanyika, Chindau, Chisanga, Chizezuru and Karanga.

Christian literature

The government's policy of education for all has created an increasingly literate population that needs reading material. The Christian church has the opportunity to meet this need with life-changing Christian literature. As the level of literacy rises, the approach and targeted audience of literature will have to be adjusted.

Apart from the section of the population which can be reached through English only, there are two categories of readers. First, there are secondary school graduates who prefer to read in English rather than a poorly translated vernacular. It is expected that this group will increase, and will need literature that is locally written and culturally acceptable.

Second, some people can only be reached effectively using a local language—about 75 percent of the population. More locally written inexpensive booklets are needed.

Most of the major centers have Christian bookshops, but foreign exchange control makes the stocking of bookshops extremely difficult unless the importer has access to foreign funds. As a result, most bookshops stock stationery and school books to subsidize the running costs of the shops. Rural areas are poorly served. A number of organizations produce Christian literature:

- Baptist Publishing House prints church-related material and will also print for other denominations.

- CAVA produces booklets and tracts, mainly in Shona.

- Christian Missions in Many Lands publishes tracts and correspondence study courses.

- Global Literature Lifeline prints correspondence courses as well as tracts and booklets.

- Mambo Press, belonging to the Catholic church, prints material for church use and publishes books written by religious or other local writers.

- Reformed Church in Zimbabwe publishes material for its own use including tracts, booklets and a Shona magazine.

- Scripture Union publishes Bible study notes.

Bible translation and distribution

The first Scripture translation into Shona was printed in 1897, when the Rev. A.A. Louw of the Dutch Reformed Mission Church published the Gospel of Mark in Chikaranga, a dialect of Shona. The New Testament was published in 1919. He also translated the Old Testament, but publication was withheld to adapt it to reach a wider number of dialects. It was not until 1950 that the whole Bible was finally produced. A second translation published in 1978 was not entirely acceptable. The Bible Society is currently working on a new translation.

The complete Bible is available in Shona, Ndebele, Chewa, Tonga, Tswana, Chivenda and in Ndau. A revision of the Ndau Bible is now in progress. The complete Ndebele Bible was published for the first time in 1978.

More people in Zimbabwe are reading the Bible, and the Bible Society reports record sales figures for 1987, selling more than 200,000 Bibles and about 17,000 New Testaments. They distributed more than 1,400,000 portions, selections, and New Reader's Scriptures.

Many of the New Reader's Scriptures went to schools and literacy classes. The Bible Society is now producing New Testaments, Scripture portions and selections locally.

Bible depots have been established in rural areas of Zimbabwe to make it easier for people living in remote localities to get Bibles and other Christian publications.

Youth in Zimbabwe have shown keen interest in a Scripture Union program recently launched for them.

Bibles for Africa has printed two million booklets containing the Gospel of Luke and the book of Acts for distribution to school children from Grade four upwards.

Christian education

Christian education in Zimbabwe is well-established. Most churches have their own theological college or Bible school. The requirements for entrance into these colleges differ. In the past, Bible schools have been willing to accept students with only a primary education, but this is changing with the government's emphasis on secondary education.

The Church in Zimbabwe needs more degree courses. The only college which offers degree courses at present is the University of Zimbabwe's Department of Theology.

The United Methodist Church is planning a university to serve their churches throughout Africa. It will offer courses at seven locations.

The Baptist Theological College is at Gweru. They have a Portuguese program for Angolan and Mozambican refugees.

The Evangelical Fellowship of Zimbabwe is investigating the possibility of establishing the Zimbabwe International School of Theology in Harare, which will offer degree courses recognized by the University of Zimbabwe.

Evangelical Bible College at Chinoyi, associated with the Evangelical Church of Zimbabwe, enrolls nearly 60 students.

Murray Theological College at Masvingo is operated by the Reformed Church in Zimbabwe.

Pentecostal Assemblies of God has a Bible college in Harare offering a three-year pastoral course. Sixty-five students from many Pentecostal churches study at this institution.

The Roman Catholic seminary is in Gweru. The Catholic church in Zimbabwe also runs three minor seminaries.

United Theological College trains ministers for the Methodist, Lutheran, Presbyterian and Independent churches.

Zimbabwe Assemblies of God has a Bible school in Harare and currently trains 120 students.

Other institutions:

- Apostolic Faith Mission Bible School in Harare
- Baptist Theological College in Gweru (Southern Baptist)
- Church of the Nazarene Bible College in Harare
- Ekuphileni Bible Institute in Bulawayo
- Lundi Bible School (Free Methodist; trains pastors and Christian workers)
- Two Lutheran Bible schools
- Mutare Bible School (Church of Christ)
- National Anglican Theological Seminary
- Rusitu Bible School (United Baptist Church)
- Solusi College in Bulawayo (Seventh Day Adventist Church)
- Wesley Bible College in Masvingo
- Zimbabwe Christian College (Churches of Christ; in Harare)

A number of these colleges and other mission groups offer correspondence courses. Bibleway correspondence courses (Southern Baptist) and Emmaus courses (Brethren) are popular.

Fambidzano is a Theological Education by Extension (TEE) college that trains church leaders from the African Independent churches. It also offers correspondence courses.

Social concerns

Churches and missions have a long history of involvement in social action. As mission stations opened in the early years, medical care and schools were established. The pioneer mission, London Missionary Society, believed that churches should be self-supporting and established development projects to create employment.

At the turn of the century, the colonial government started making small contributions towards the cost of education. By 1947, the government had assumed full responsibility for the salaries of all qualified teachers in mission schools. Today, mission schools constitute about 10 percent of the education system. Salaries are still paid by the government, but churches retain the right to employ Christian teachers. Nearly three million school children receive religious education that is biblical in content.

The government began subsidizing medical work in 1927. At that time, five doctors and 21 nurses worked in the country. With financial assistance from the government, 15 more mission hospitals were started between 1928 and 1930. Today, mission hospitals are fully funded by the government. Missions and churches involved in health care include:

- Anglican church
- Baptist Convention of Zimbabwe
- Elim Mission
- Evangelical Lutheran Church in Zimbabwe
- Free Methodist Church
- Reformed Church of Zambia
- Roman Catholic Church
- Salvation Army
- Seventh Day Adventists
- TEAM
- United Church of Christ in Zambia
- United Methodist Church

The majority of churches, missions, and parachurch organizations are involved in social action, and community development is encouraged by the government.

Christian Care is the relief and development agency of the Zimbabwe Christian Council. Salvation Army cares for the aged in four homes, operates hostels for girls, and runs training farms and educational centers. World Vision is involved in childcare and has 76 community development projects. Other agencies involved with social concerns include Baptist World Relief, Catholic Relief Services, and Lutheran World Federation.

About 1,000 non-governmental organizations are registered with the government, and include organizations such as The Hunger Project, Oxfam U.K., CUSO, and many local social services.

About 175,000 Mozambican refugees are cared for in five different camps in Zimbabwe.

SPECIAL NEEDS IN ZIMBABWE

- Pastors want further education so they can confidently minister to an emerging well-educated generation.
- Leaders face the challenge of guiding churches in evangelistic outreach and coping with issues like ancestor veneration.
- Rural people are isolated and difficult to reach. Many left churches to return to traditionalism during the war years.
- The church hopes to build rapport with the government and be outspoken when necessary.
- Cross-cultural reconciliation and relationship-building are needed to heal the hurts and polarization still existing between the different races.
- The majority of the population (59%) is under 20 years of age.
- Newly literate people need Christian publications.
- Expatriates require a deep understanding of indigenous culture to appreciate the difficulties facing Christians in Zimbabwe.
- People in the process of modernization, dislocated from their rural traditions, may be more open to Christianity.

BIBLIOGRAPHY

Africa South of the Sahara, Europa Publications.

Dodge, A.E., *Historical Overview of North American Protestant Missions*, Yale Divinity School.

Economist Intelligence Unit, *Zimbabwe Country Profile 1990/91*.

Economist Intelligence Unit, *EIU Country Report No. 1, 1991*.

First Five-year National Development Plan 1986-1990.

Hawkins, Tony, *Zimbabwe's Socialist Transformation*, Optima.

Kapenyi, Geoffrey Z., *The Clash of Cultures: Christian Missionaries and the Shona of Rhodesia*, University Press of America.

King, P.S., *Missions in Southern Rhodesia*, Inyati Centenary Trust.

Kongwa, Sam, *Zimbabwe: The Socialist State*, Africa Institute Bulletin No. 5, 1987.

Randolph R.H., *Church and State in Rhodesia*, 1869-1971.

Smith, Edwin W., *The Way of the White Fields*, Dominion Press.

Statistical Yearbook of Zimbabwe 1987, Central Statistical Office, Ministry of Information.

United Bible Societies, *World Annual Report*, 1987.

van der Merwe, T. and Groenewald B.H., *Christian Literature in Zimbabwe*, Paper from Conference at Potchefstroom University for Christian Higher Education.

van der Merwe, W.J., *From Mission Field to Autonomous Church in Zimbabwe*, NG Kerk Boekhandel.

van der Merwe, W.J., *The Witness of the Church in Zimbabwe*, Lovedale Press, 1982.

Weller, John and Linden, Jane, *Mainstream Christianity to 1980 in Malawi, Zambia and Zimbabwe*, Mambo Press.